DRESSING UP
WITHDRAW FUN

Rebekah Joy Shirley
Photography by Chris Fairclough

This edition published in 2011 by Arcturus Publishing Limited
26/27 Bickels Yard, 151–153 Bermondsey Street,
London SE1 3HA

ISBN: 978-1-84837-915-2
CH001886EN
Supplier 05, Date 0911, Print run 966

Printed in Singapore

Editor for Arcturus Publishing: Joe Harris
Designer: Emma Randall
Cover design: Peter Ridley

Managing editor for Discovery Books: Laura Durman
Editor: Rebecca Hunter
Designer: Blink Media
Photography: Chris Fairclough

The author and photographer would like to acknowledge the following for their help in
preparing this book: the staff and pupils of Chad Vale Primary School, Amelia Adams, Iqrah
Choudhury, Malachi Clearkin, Jack Coady, Cyrus Dhariwal, Suchir Gella, Avneet Gill, Ayla-
Belma Hadzovic, Ryan Hudson, Zaydan Law, Sunny Marko-Bennett, Rory Munro, Rosie
Palmer-Downes, Abbie Sangha, Oliver Town, Wasiq Ul-Islam, Charlie Walker, Sharnai
Walker, Anton Walters, Annia J Wright and Lydia Wright.

NOTE TO PARENTS
Some of the projects in this book may require the use of craft knives, needles and pins.
We would advise that young children are supervised by a responsible adult.

CONTENTS

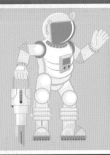

DRESSING UP AS AN

In this chapter you will be transformed into a space cadet exploring the universe. Learn how to make a spacesuit and helmet, space boots and gloves and even your own alien friend!

ASTRONAUT

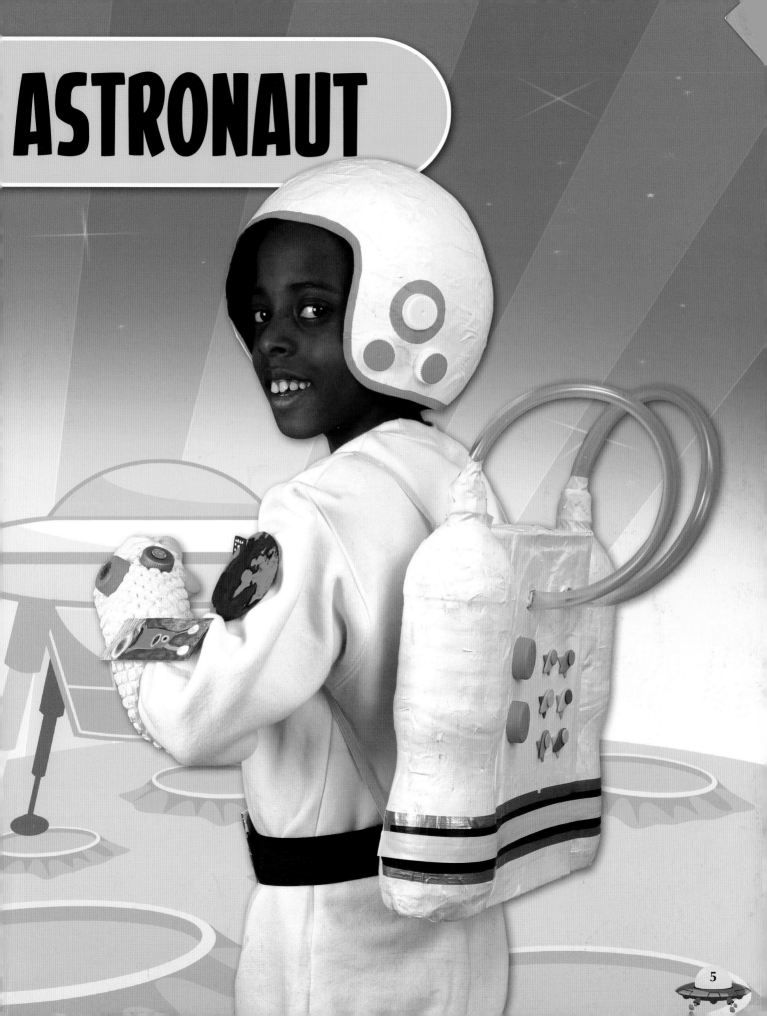

A SUIT FOR SPACE

An astronaut's space suit is covered in many bright badges. You can decorate yours with different designs. You will also need an ID badge!

To make and decorate your suit you will need:
A white sweatshirt
A pair of white trousers
Cardboard
Coloured paints and a paintbrush
Craft gems
Foam shapes
Craft glue and a paintbrush
A pair of scissors
A photo of yourself
Safety pins
White paper
Coloured tape and sticky tape
A pen
A ruler

1 Cut out a circle and a rocket shape from cardboard and paint them bright colours.

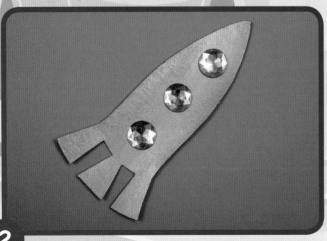

2 Glue gems down the middle of the rocket shape to look like windows.

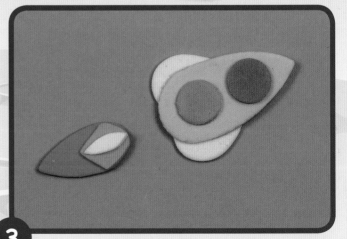

3 Cut out foam shapes to make your own space design.

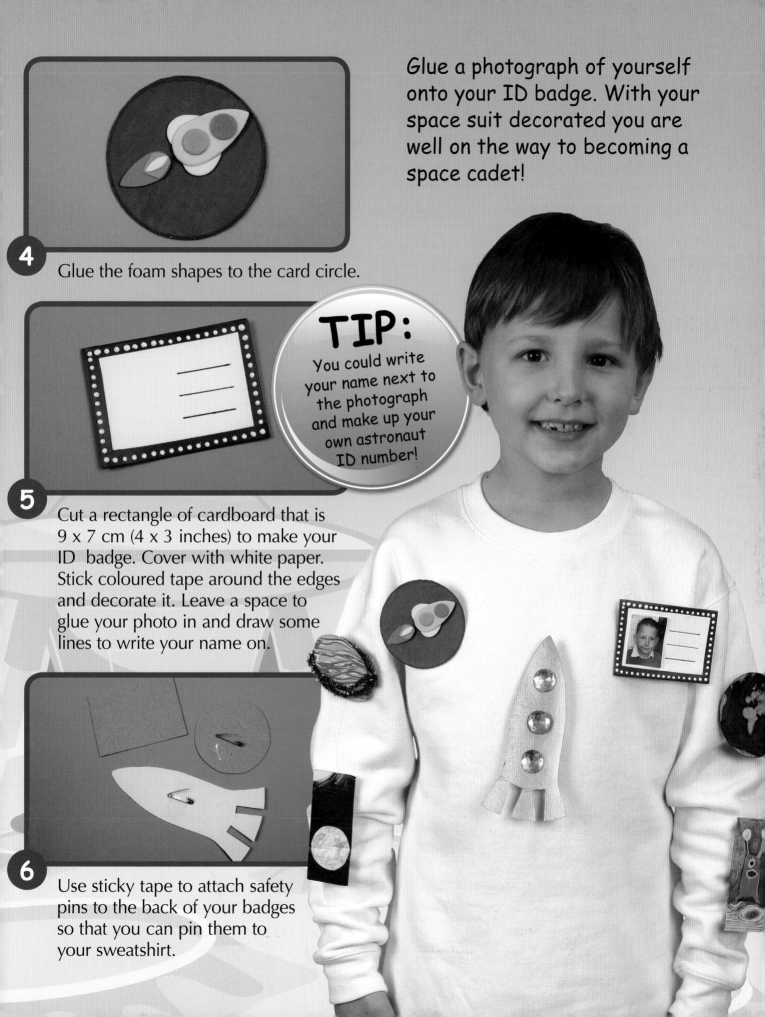

Glue a photograph of yourself onto your ID badge. With your space suit decorated you are well on the way to becoming a space cadet!

4 Glue the foam shapes to the card circle.

TIP:
You could write your name next to the photograph and make up your own astronaut ID number!

5 Cut a rectangle of cardboard that is 9 x 7 cm (4 x 3 inches) to make your ID badge. Cover with white paper. Stick coloured tape around the edges and decorate it. Leave a space to glue your photo in and draw some lines to write your name on.

6 Use sticky tape to attach safety pins to the back of your badges so that you can pin them to your sweatshirt.

A HIGH-TECH HELMET

Astronauts need to wear protective helmets when they go into space. The helmet must be able to survive very hot and cold temperatures.

1 Measure around your head with a tape measure. Blow up a balloon so that it is slightly bigger than your head measurement.

3 When the glue is dry, burst the balloon and paint the dome white.

2 Glue the newspaper strips to the top part of the balloon. Cover it with about three layers of newspaper.

TIP:
If you want to make the glue runnier, mix four teaspoons of water with two tablespoons of craft glue in a jam jar.

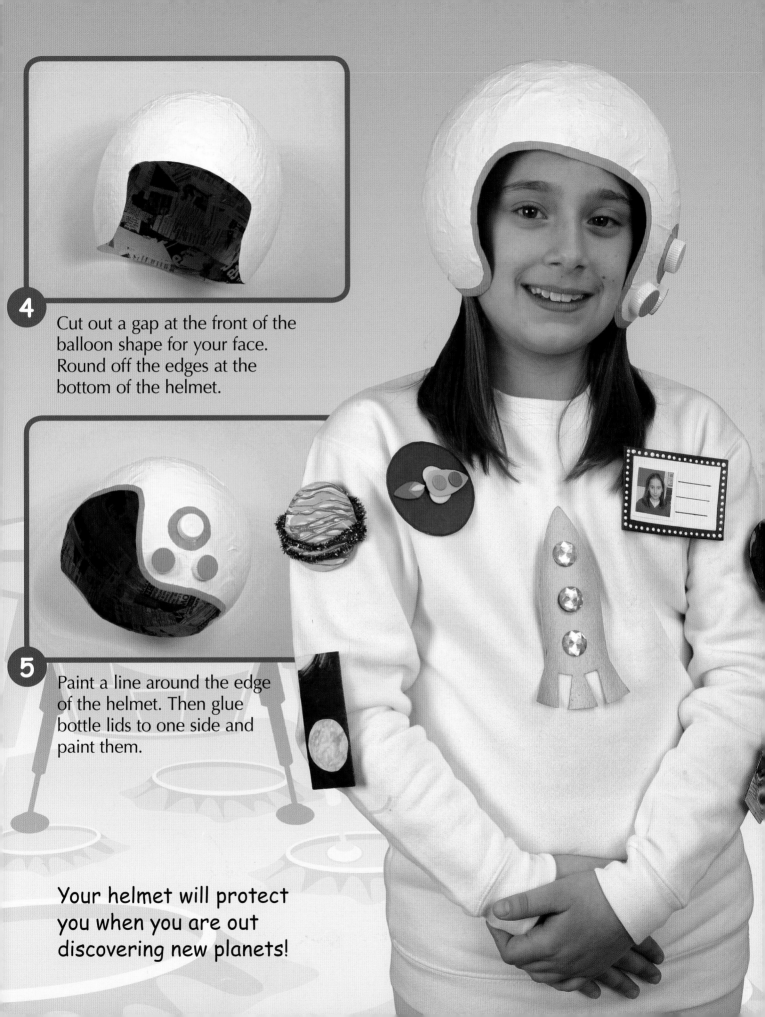

4

Cut out a gap at the front of the balloon shape for your face. Round off the edges at the bottom of the helmet.

5

Paint a line around the edge of the helmet. Then glue bottle lids to one side and paint them.

Your helmet will protect you when you are out discovering new planets!

SPACE BOOTS AND EQUIPMENT BELT

An astronaut's job is to explore the solar system. Astronauts must wear special boots to walk on the surface of new planets. They need to wear a special belt to carry all their equipment, too.

To make your own space boots and belt you will need:
A pair of wellington boots
Metallic paint and a paintbrush
Coloured tape
A tape measure
A strip of wide elastic or stretchy fabric, about 1m (3 feet) long
Cardboard
Velcro
Craft glue and a paintbrush
A pair of scissors
A craft knife
Silver foil
Coloured foam squares

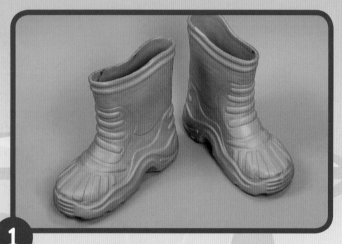

1 Paint the boots with metallic paint. You may need a few coats of paint.

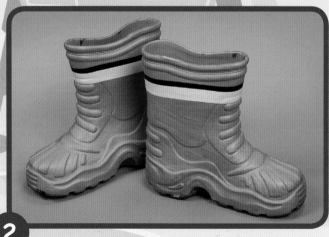

2 Stick coloured tape around the top of the boots.

3 Measure your waist with a tape measure. Cut a strip of elastic or stretchy fabric that is 3 cm (1 inch) longer than your waist measurement.

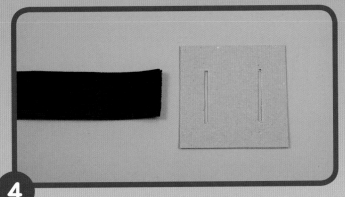

4 Cut out a piece of cardboard about 8 cm (3 inches) square. To make the buckle, cut two slits in the cardboard using a craft knife. The slits should be about 2 cm (½ inch) from each side and as long as the width of the elastic you are using for your belt.

You are almost ready to set out on your journey to explore new worlds. You can add all sorts of space equipment to your belt!

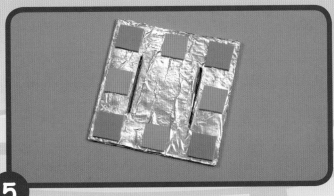

5 Glue silver foil onto the cardboard buckle. When the glue is dry, cut through the slits. Decorate the buckle with coloured foam squares.

6 Thread the elastic through the buckle and glue a small piece of Velcro to each end so you can fasten your belt.

GATHERING MOON DUST

Astronauts collect samples from the planets to send to scientists back on Earth. They need to wear special gloves to protect their hands.

To make your space gloves and sample jars you will need:
Small, empty jam jars
Glitter, cotton wool balls, beads and craft pompoms
Sticky labels
A ruler
Bubble wrap
White paint and a paintbrush
Four plastic bottle tops
Sequins
Craft glue and a paintbrush
A pair of scissors
White cotton gloves
Coloured paints and a paintbrush
Coloured pens or pencils
Velcro

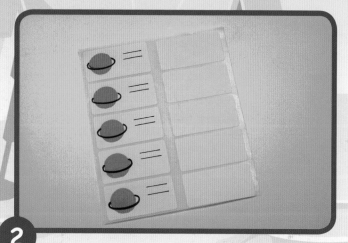

1 Fill the jam jars with brightly coloured things such as beads and glitter, or craft pompoms and cotton wool balls. Paint the lids different colours.

2 Design a logo and draw it on the sticky labels. Draw lines with a ruler on the labels so you can write which planet your samples came from.

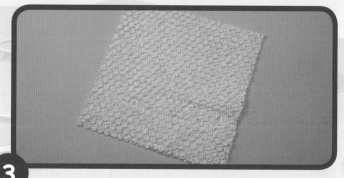

3 Cut out two pieces of bubble wrap about 24 cm (10 inches) square. Paint them white.

Put your gloves on and then attach the bubble wrap squares over the top using the Velcro. Now you are ready to go out and collect lots of interesting things from space!

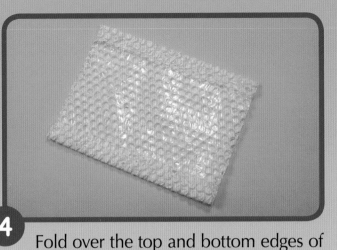

4 Fold over the top and bottom edges of each piece and glue in place.

5 Cut a strip of Velcro about 20 cm (8 inches) long. Glue one half along the top of each bubble wrap square. Glue the other half along the bottom of each square.

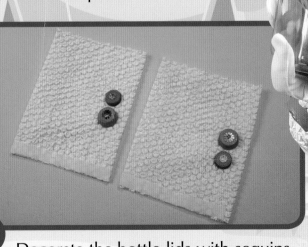

6 Decorate the bottle lids with sequins. Glue two bottle lids on the top of each square in the middle of one edge.

ASTRO PACK

Astronauts carry space packs on their backs. A space pack contains oxygen to help them breathe on other planets.

Make a space pack using:
Coloured electrical tape
2 large empty plastic bottles
A large cereal packet
1m (40 inch) length of clear plastic pipe
White paint and a paintbrush
1m (40 inch) length of white elastic
Newspaper, torn into strips
Sticky tape
Craft glue and a paintbrush
Foam shapes
A pair of scissors

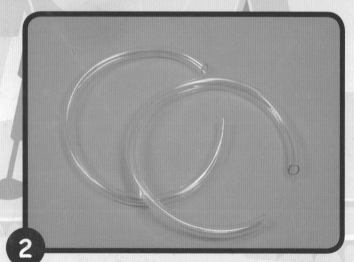

1 Attach the bottles either side of the cereal packet using sticky tape.

2 Using scissors, cut the plastic pipe in half so that you have two 50 cm (20 inch) lengths.

3 Insert one end of each pipe into the necks of the bottles. Use sticky tape to secure the pipes.

4 Make holes in the back of the cereal packet and push the other ends of the pipes into them.

5 Cut the elastic in half. Use sticky tape to attach one end of the elastic pieces to the top corners of the cereal packet, and the other ends to the bottom corners.

Now you are ready to step out onto strange new planets. Beware of aliens!

TIP:
If you want to make the glue runnier, mix four teaspoons of water with two tablespoons of craft glue in a jam jar.

6 Cover the packet and bottles in four layers of newspaper strips and glue.

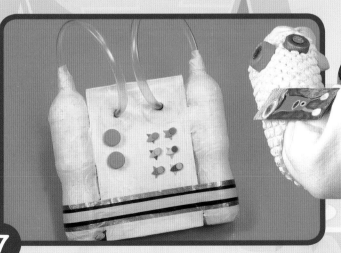

7 Paint the space pack white and decorate it with coloured electrical tape and foam shapes.

SPACE SPEAK

When astronauts are exploring planets they need to talk with their spaceship and also with scientists on Earth. They need a space radio to do this.

Make your space radio using:
Cardboard
Newspaper, torn into strips
Coloured paints and a paintbrush
Sequins
A plastic straw
A polystyrene ball
Three plastic bottle lids
A jar lid
Craft glue and a paintbrush
Elastic
Split pins
A pair of scissors
A permanent marker pen
A ruler
A pen or pencil

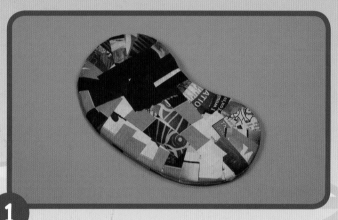

1 Draw two bean shapes on cardboard and cut them out. Glue them together and then cover them with strips of newspaper and glue. Continue until your space radio is nice and sturdy.

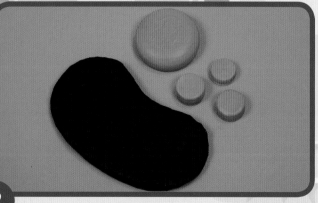

2 Paint the card shape. Then paint a jar lid and three bottle lids in a different colour.

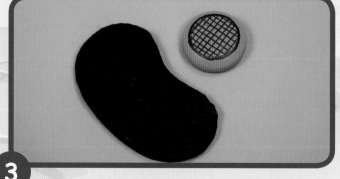

3 Use a ruler and marker pen to draw lines across the jar lid from side to side and then from top to bottom. This will make a criss-cross pattern.

4 Glue the lids to the bean shape. Decorate with sequins.

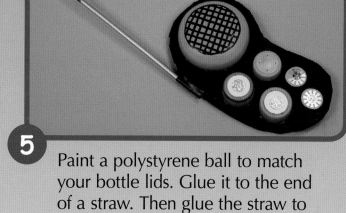

5 Paint a polystyrene ball to match your bottle lids. Glue it to the end of a straw. Then glue the straw to the side of the bean shape.

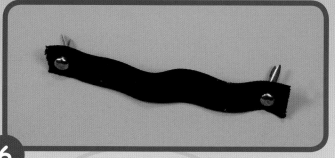

6 Cut a piece of elastic that is 2 cm (1 inch) wider than the middle of your space radio. Push split pins through the elastic around 1 cm (½ inch) from each end.

7 Push the split pins through your tool belt and open them. You can now tuck your space radio into your tool belt.

Now you can talk to your fellow astronauts wherever you are in space!

ALIEN LIFE DETECTOR

When you land on another planet, one of the first things you need to do is see if anything lives there. This alien life detector will do the job.

To make your own detector you will need:
A 35 cm (14 inch) length of dowel
Coloured card
Coloured tape
Two polystyrene balls
A metallic pipe cleaner
Craft glue and a paintbrush
A pair of scissors
A biro
Coloured paint and a paintbrush
A compass
A pen or pencil
A ruler

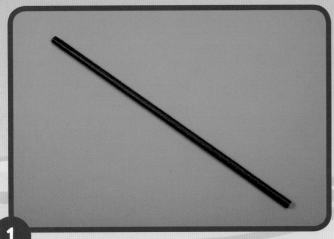

1 Cover the dowel in coloured tape.

TIP: You could use a compass to draw the circles.

2 Draw six circles onto coloured card and cut them out. Make a hole in each one by pushing a biro through the middle.

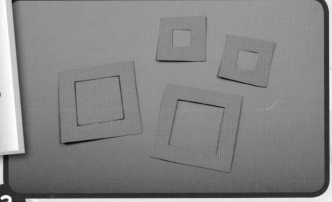

3 Draw two 12 cm (5 inch) squares and two 10 cm (4 inch) squares onto coloured card. Cut the squares out. Then draw a smaller square inside each one and cut them out, too.

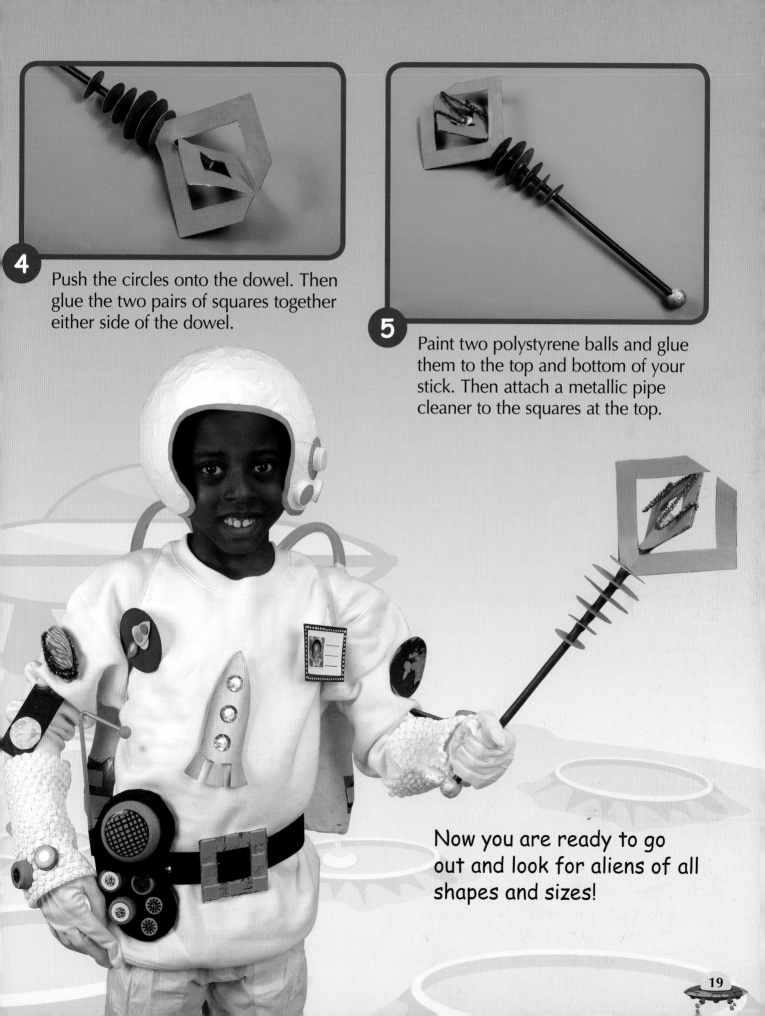

4 Push the circles onto the dowel. Then glue the two pairs of squares together either side of the dowel.

5 Paint two polystyrene balls and glue them to the top and bottom of your stick. Then attach a metallic pipe cleaner to the squares at the top.

Now you are ready to go out and look for aliens of all shapes and sizes!

DO YOU BELIEVE IN ALIENS?

If you find a friendly alien, you might keep it with you as a pet.

Make your own alien friend using:
A green sock
Green pipe cleaners
Two polystyrene balls
Stuffing or old pairs of tights
Craft glue and a paintbrush
A plastic eye
Paint and a paintbrush
A pair of scissors

1 Use scissors to carefully snip two small slits on each side of the toe end of the sock. Push a green pipe cleaner through the slits.

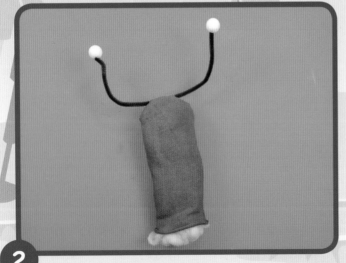

2 Push a polystyrene ball onto each end of the pipe cleaner. Stuff the sock with stuffing or pairs of tights.

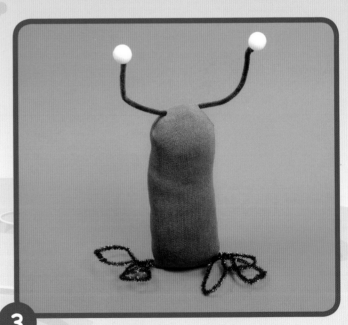

3 Place a pipe cleaner across the open end of the sock and glue the gap up. Bend the pipe cleaner to make feet shapes.

Your alien friend will be able to tell you lots of things about life in outer space.

4 Glue a plastic eye in the middle of the alien's head and paint a mouth shape under it.

FLY THE FLAG

Astronauts use flags to mark the places that they have visited in the universe. You could put your name or initials on your flag so people know what a great explorer you are!

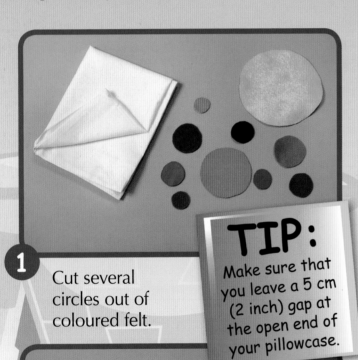

1 Cut several circles out of coloured felt.

TIP: Make sure that you leave a 5 cm (2 inch) gap at the open end of your pillowcase.

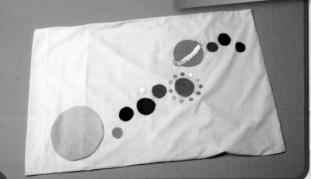

2 Glue the circles to the pillowcase. Add some foiled paper rings and sequins.

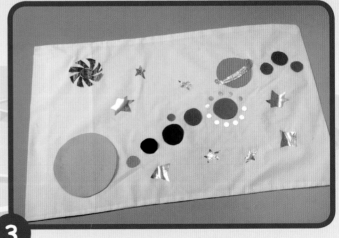

3 Draw some stars and other space shapes on foiled paper. Cut them out and glue them to the pillowcase.

4 Wrap some coloured tape around the cane. Paint a polystyrene ball and glue it to the end of the cane.

5 Fold 3 cm (1 inch) of the open edge of the pillowcase over. Use scissors to snip small semicircles along the fold.

With your space-age flag you are really ready to conquer the universe!

6 Guide the cane through the holes in the pillowcase and glue in place.

DRESSING UP AS A

In this chapter you will be transformed into a fairy of the forest, complete with wings and a bouquet of wild flowers. With your fairy wand you can grant wishes to all your woodland friends!

FAIRY

A FAIRYTALE DRESS

Making a costume can be messy work! Make sure you cover all surfaces with newspaper before you start.

Woodland fairies live in a secret world of their own. They wear clothes made from leaves and flowers.

To make a forest fairy outfit you will need:
An old vest or t-shirt
A bin liner (preferably green)
Coloured plastic bags (preferably green, yellow and orange)
1m (40 inches) length of green ribbon
Sticky tape
A pair of scissors
A needle and thread
A ruler

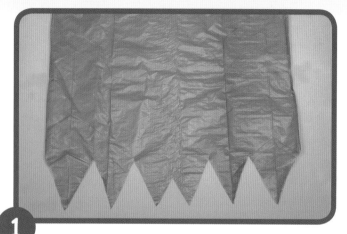

1 Cut the bin liner to the length you want your skirt to be. Cut triangles out of the bottom edge.

2 Cut two slits in the middle at the top of the bag. The slits should be about 5 cm (2 inches) apart and 3 cm (1 inch) from the top of the bag. Pull the ends of the ribbon through the slits you have made. The ribbon ends should be inside the bag.

3 Fold the top edge of the bag over so that the ribbon is hidden and the ends are now outside the bag. Stick tape along the edge to hold it in place.

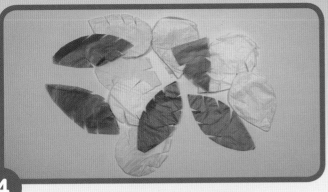

4 Cut leaf shapes out of different coloured carrier bags.

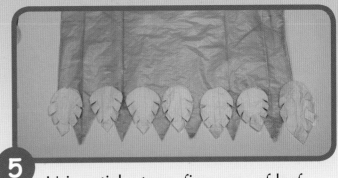

5 Using sticky tape, fix a row of leaf shapes at the bottom of the bin liner.

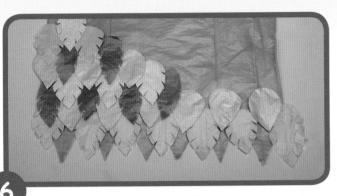

6 Stick another row of leaves above the first row, overlapping it slightly. Continue adding rows until the bag is covered.

7 Sew the leaf shapes around the top of your vest, using two or three stitches at the top of each leaf.

Carefully put on your fairy top. Then tie the ribbon around your waist to wear your skirt. You're ready to play in the forest!

FLUTTERING WINGS

Fairies fly using their beautiful, sparkly wings. Fairy wings are very fragile and must be handled with care.

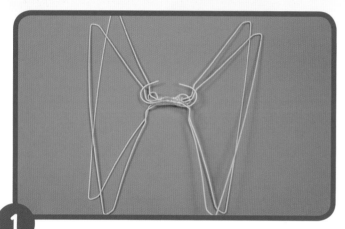

1 Take two coat hangers and join them at the twisted part by the hooks. Use sticky tape to secure. Then attach the other two coat hangers on top of them, leaving two hooks sticking out.

2 Cut the top off the pair of tights. Cut each leg in half.

3 Stretch these four pieces over the wire wing-shapes and tie at the back. Ask an adult to straighten the hooks.

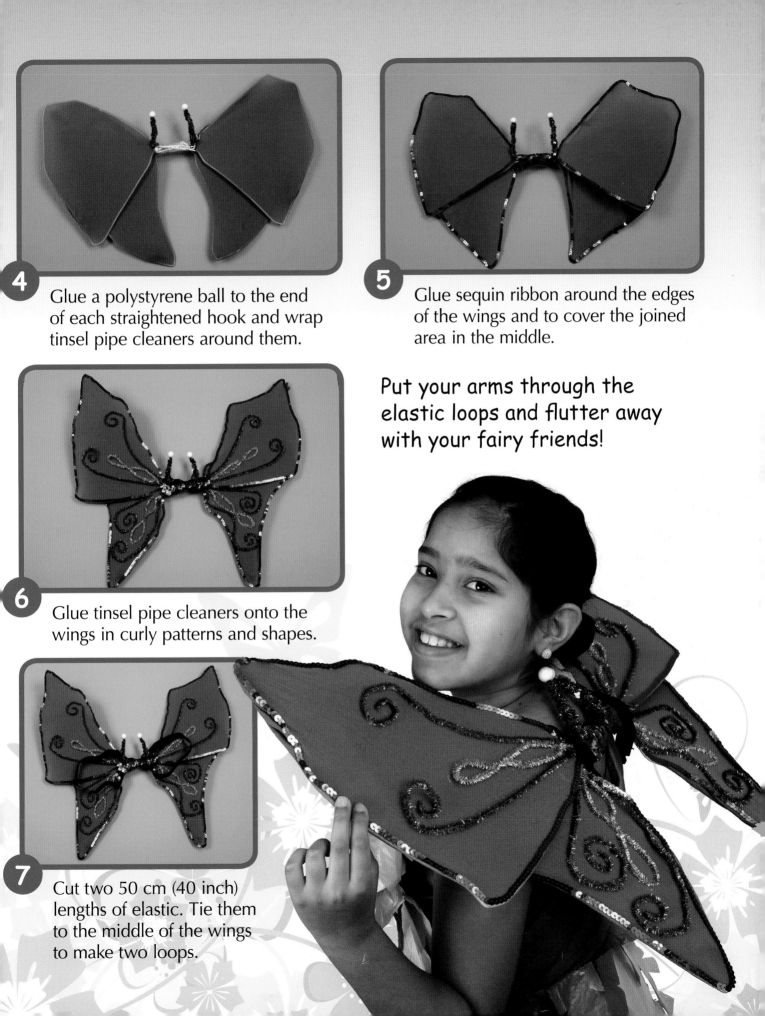

4 Glue a polystyrene ball to the end of each straightened hook and wrap tinsel pipe cleaners around them.

5 Glue sequin ribbon around the edges of the wings and to cover the joined area in the middle.

Put your arms through the elastic loops and flutter away with your fairy friends!

6 Glue tinsel pipe cleaners onto the wings in curly patterns and shapes.

7 Cut two 50 cm (40 inch) lengths of elastic. Tie them to the middle of the wings to make two loops.

FAIRY FEET

Fairies wear beautiful, dainty shoes on their feet so that they can skip silently through the forest.

Make your own fairy slippers using:
Fun foam
A hole punch
Ten lengths of ribbon, each about 50 cm (20 inches) long, in different colours
A pair of scissors
A ruler
A pen or pencil

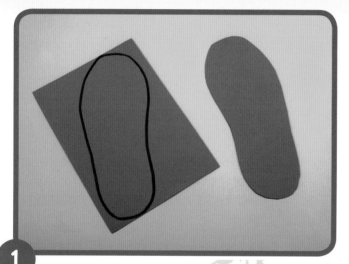

1 Draw around a pair of your shoes on a piece of fun foam. Then cut the shapes out.

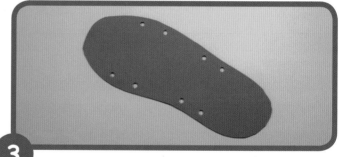

3 Punch four holes towards the back of each shoe as shown above.

TIP:
If the foam is too thick to use a hole punch, ask an adult to make the holes in the foam for you.

2 Punch four holes at the front of each shoe as shown in the picture. The holes should be about 3 cm (1 inch) apart and 1 cm (½ inch) from the edge.

4 Tie three ribbons together with a knot at each end. Thread the ribbons through the front holes in a criss-cross pattern.

5

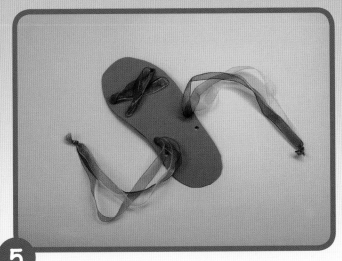

Bring the ends of the ribbons up through the front two holes at the back of the shoe.

6

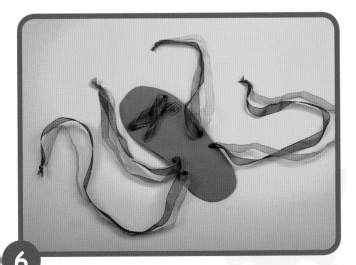

Take two more ribbons and thread them through the two holes at the very back of each shoe. Then tie a knot at the ends.

Tie the ribbons in a criss-cross way finishing with a bow at the back of your leg. Now you are ready to skip through the forest in your fantastic fairy footwear.

FLOWERS FOR A FAIRY

Fairies love to gather flowers from the forests and meadows. Make this bunch of flowers to show your fairy friends, and add a little ladybird friend.

To make your flowers and ladybird you will need:
Coloured tissue paper
Green pipe cleaners
A pair of scissors
Red and black felt
Two plastic eyes
Craft glue and a paintbrush
A ruler

1 Cut the tissue paper into rectangles about 6 x 16 cm (2 x 6 inches).

TIP: For smaller flowers make smaller rectangles.

2 Fold each piece of tissue paper backwards and forwards down the length of the rectangle until the whole paper is folded up. Then tie one end of a pipe cleaner around the middle.

3 Trim the ends of the tissue paper strip. You could cut the end into a point or a rounded shape.

4 Gently spread out the paper folds on both sides to make a flower shape. Repeat to make a whole bouquet.

Glue the ladybird onto a flower. Carry your beautiful flowers with you wherever you go. You could also use them to decorate your hair, clothing and shoes.

5

Cut a circle of red felt about 3 cm (1 inch) in diameter. Also cut out an oval of black felt and four small circles.

6

Glue them all to the red circle.

7

Glue two plastic eyes to the ladybird.

A 'MAKE-A-WISH' WAND

Fairies carry a magic wand with them wherever they go. They use the wand to grant wishes.

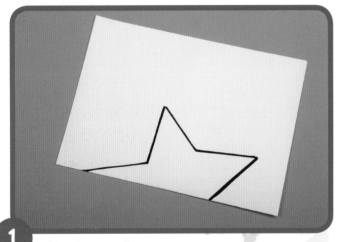

1 Fold a piece of card in half. Use a ruler to draw half a star onto the card along the fold.

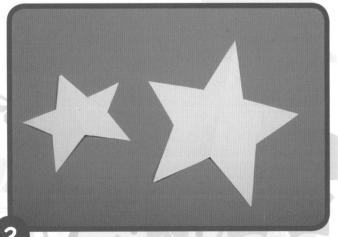

2 Cut out the shape and unfold the star. Then draw a smaller star in the same way.

3 Draw around the star shapes on metallic foiled paper. Cut the shapes out.

4 Glue the metallic paper onto the card stars and glue the stars together. Decorate with craft gems and sequins.

5 Glue one end of the ribbon to the bottom of the dowel. Wrap the ribbon around the dowel and tape it at the end.

6 Use strong sticky tape to attach the dowel to the back of the star.

Now wave your wand and make someone's dream come true. Whose wish will you grant first?

A HEAVENLY HEADBAND

Woodland fairies wear beautiful headbands made of forest vines, leaves and flowers.

Make your own forest headband using:
Green pipe cleaners
Green paper or plastic
Craft glue and a paintbrush
Coloured tissue paper
A pair of scissors

1 Make a crown as the base of your headband by wrapping ten pipe cleaners around each other to form a circle. The circle needs to fit comfortably on your head.

2 Cut some leaf shapes out of green paper or plastic.

3 Make some small paper flowers in the same way as you did on page 32.

4

Twist the pipe cleaners to add the flowers to your headband. Then glue the leaves to the headband.

TIP:
Perhaps you could add other colourful things to your headband.

With your headband in place you will look like a fairy queen with a tiara!

37

JOLLY JEWELLERY

Fairies always look beautiful. They wear jewellery made from forest treasures around their necks, wrists and ankles.

Make a bracelet and necklace using:
String, wool and ribbon
Thread
A pair of scissors
Pipe cleaners
Craft feathers
A ruler

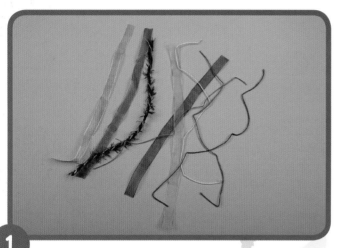

1 Cut several lengths of string, wool and ribbon. They should be long enough to fit around your wrist.

2 Twist the lengths together around a pipe cleaner and tie in place. Tie on some feathers using thread.

3 Twist the ends of the pipe cleaner together to make the bracelet. You can alter it to make it fit your wrist.

You can make several bracelets in different colours. Tie some around your ankles. Now you are ready to frolic in the forest with your fairy friends!

4 Cut six 1m (40 inch) lengths of string, wool, ribbon and thread.

5 Twist the lengths together, adding feathers as before. Leave two long ribbons for tying.

6 Tie the ends of the necklace in a bow.

A FLUTTERING FRIEND

Fairies make friends easily with the creatures that surround them. They particularly love playing with the beautiful butterflies that flutter through the forest.

Make your own butterfly companion using:
9 tinsel pipe cleaners
A pair of scissors
Metallic card
Craft gems
Glitter glue
Sticky tape
A ruler
Craft glue and a paintbrush

1 Take two pipe cleaners and wrap the ends around your finger a couple of times to make the antennae of your butterfly.

2 Use six pipe cleaners for the body of the butterfly. Join these to the antennae by wrapping another pipe cleaner around them. The antennae should stick out at the front.

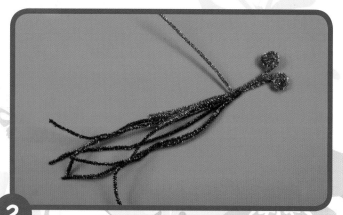

3 Pull two of the pipe cleaners in the bundle out to one side. Wrap the ends back around the body to make loops for wings.

4 Repeat to make two wing shapes on the other side. Then pull another pipe cleaner out on each side and leave them loose.

5 Continue wrapping the pipe cleaner from step 2 around the body until it is 10 cm (4 inches) long. Cut off the end.

Use the two loose pipe cleaners to attach the butterfly to your arm. What a beautiful fairy friend!

6 Cut out four wing shapes from metallic card and decorate them with glitter glue and craft gems.

7 Use sticky tape to attach the card wings to the pipe cleaner loops.

A FAIRY'S BEST FRIEND

Some of the fairies' best friends are the elves that live in the forest. Elves are very mischievous and love to play games and have fun.

TIP:
You could follow the instructions for the fairy dress to cover your elf t-shirt in leaves if you like.

1 Cut triangles out of the bottom of the t-shirt. Cut triangles along the sleeve edges, too.

2 Measure round your waist with a tape measure. Cut a strip of brown felt that is 5 cm (2 inches) wide and 20 cm (8 inches) longer than your waist.

3 Cut out a circle of brown felt about 50 cm (20 inches) across. Cut triangles around the edge.

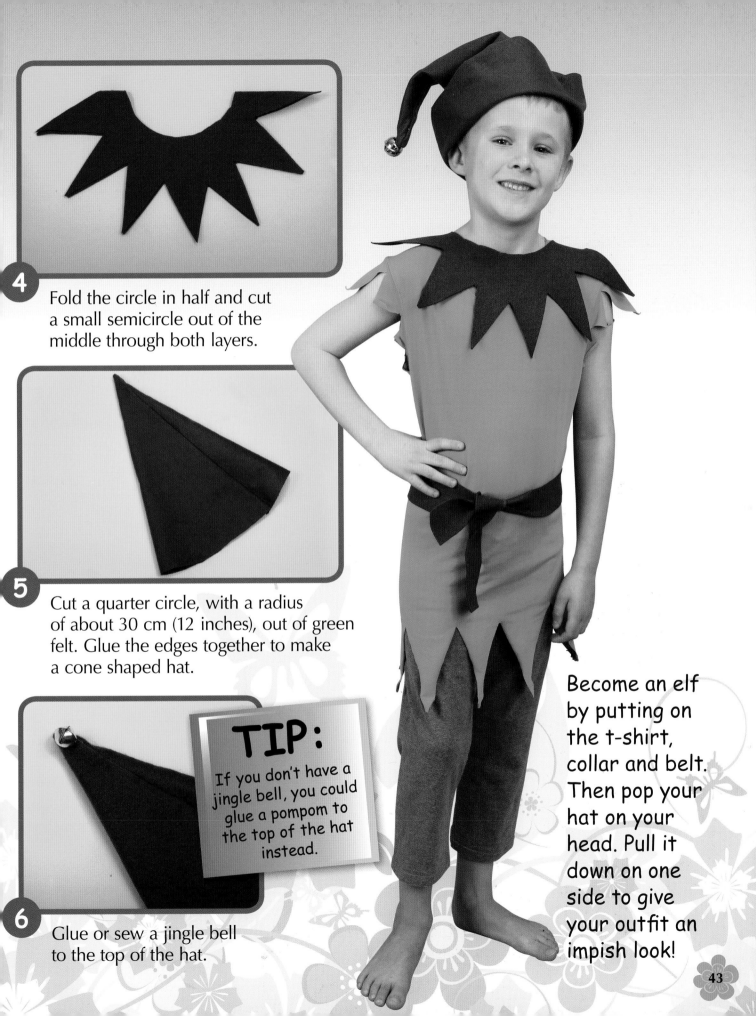

4 Fold the circle in half and cut a small semicircle out of the middle through both layers.

5 Cut a quarter circle, with a radius of about 30 cm (12 inches), out of green felt. Glue the edges together to make a cone shaped hat.

TIP:
If you don't have a jingle bell, you could glue a pompom to the top of the hat instead.

6 Glue or sew a jingle bell to the top of the hat.

Become an elf by putting on the t-shirt, collar and belt. Then pop your hat on your head. Pull it down on one side to give your outfit an impish look!

DRESSING UP AS A

This chapter shows you how to make a costume fit for fighting a dragon or jousting in a tournament. Learn how to construct a suit of armour, a lance and a sword, and how to decorate your shield with a coat of arms.

KNIGHT

KEEP YOUR HEAD!

Making a costume can be messy work! Make sure you cover all surfaces with newspaper before you start.

Knights often fought on the battlefield. They had to protect themselves from enemies. Knights needed helmets to protect their heads.

Make a helmet using:
A balloon
A tape measure
Newspaper, torn into strips
Craft glue and a paintbrush
Silver paint and a paintbrush
Silver sequins
Silver fabric
An old cereal packet
A pair of scissors
A ruler

TIP:
If you want to make the glue runnier, mix four teaspoons of water with two tablespoons of glue in a jam jar.

1 Measure around your head with a tape measure. Blow up a balloon so that it is slightly bigger than your head measurement. Cover the top half of the balloon in three layers of newspaper and glue.

2 When the glue is dry, burst the balloon. Tidy the edges of the dome and paint it silver.

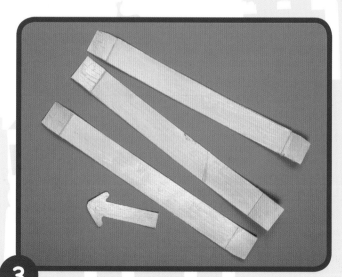

3 Cut three strips of card 30 x 5 cm (12 x 2 inches) from a cereal packet. Cut an arrow-shaped nose guard from the card, too. Paint all the pieces of card silver.

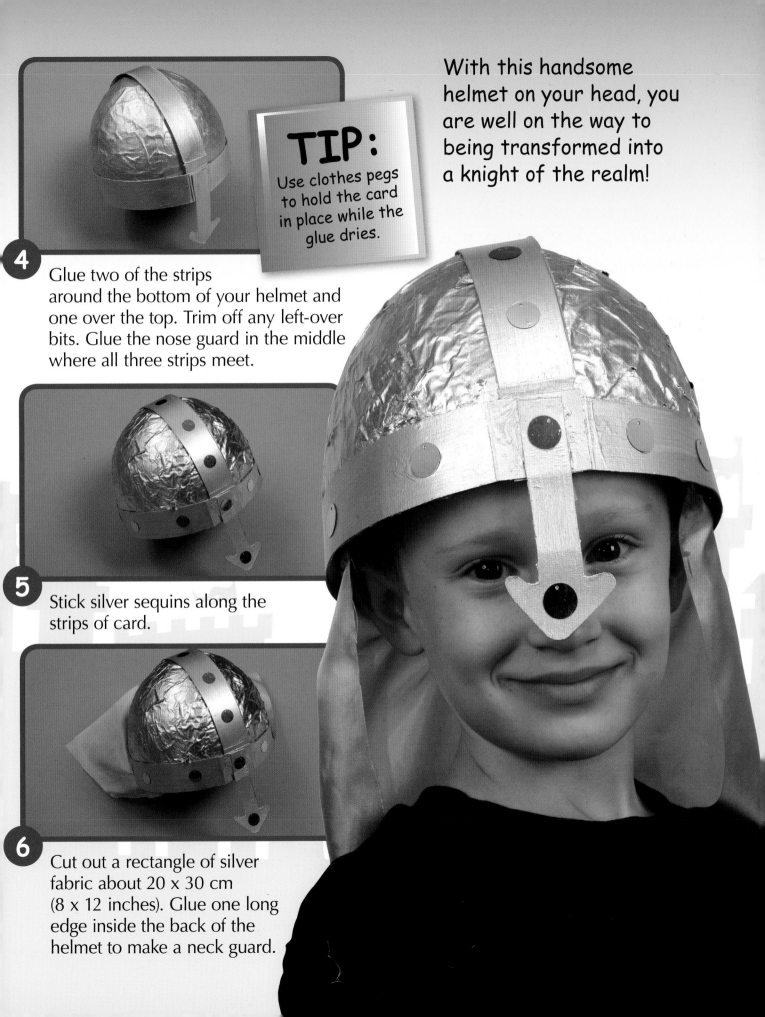

With this handsome helmet on your head, you are well on the way to being transformed into a knight of the realm!

TIP:
Use clothes pegs to hold the card in place while the glue dries.

4 Glue two of the strips around the bottom of your helmet and one over the top. Trim off any left-over bits. Glue the nose guard in the middle where all three strips meet.

5 Stick silver sequins along the strips of card.

6 Cut out a rectangle of silver fabric about 20 x 30 cm (8 x 12 inches). Glue one long edge inside the back of the helmet to make a neck guard.

BEST IN THE VEST!

Knights wore protective vests made of chain mail. Chain mail is made from iron rings linked together in rows.

To make your own chain mail vest you will need:
An old, grey long-sleeved t-shirt
A black permanent marker pen
A large plastic bottle top
Newspaper

1 Draw around the bottle top in black marker pen to make a curved row of circles on the t-shirt.

TIP:
Put two sheets of newspaper inside your t-shirt to stop the marker pen leaking through to the other side.

2 Draw another row of circles overlapping the first.

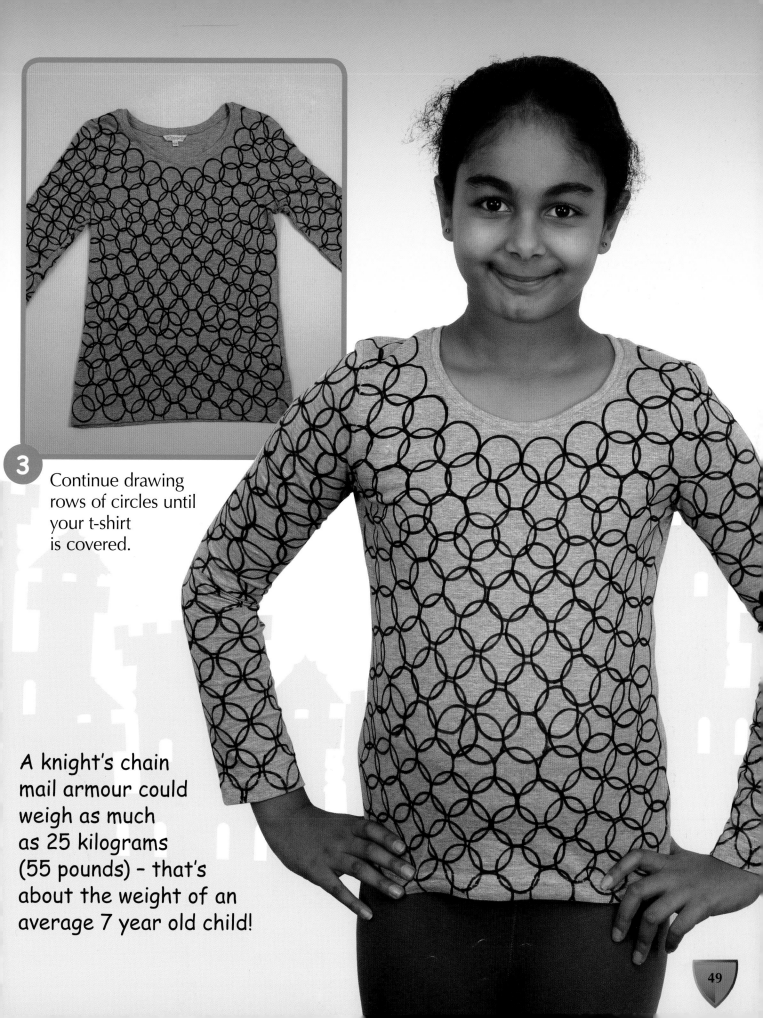

3

Continue drawing
rows of circles until
your t-shirt
is covered.

A knight's chain
mail armour could
weigh as much
as 25 kilograms
(55 pounds) – that's
about the weight of an
average 7 year old child!

A KNIGHT IN SHINING ARMOUR

A knight's arms, legs, shoulders, elbows and knees were protected by large pieces of metal called plate armour.

Make plate armour using:
Four large plastic bottles
A craft knife
Six paper dust masks
Silver paint and a paintbrush
Elastic
A pair of scissors
A hole punch

1 Ask an adult to cut the tops and bottoms off four plastic bottles to make plastic tubes.

2 Cut the tubes in half lengthways and paint them silver.

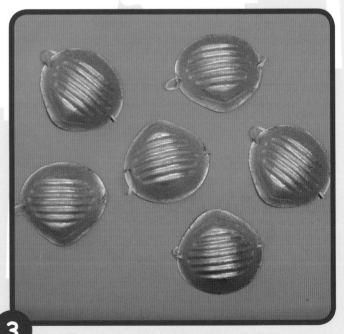

3 Paint the dust masks silver.

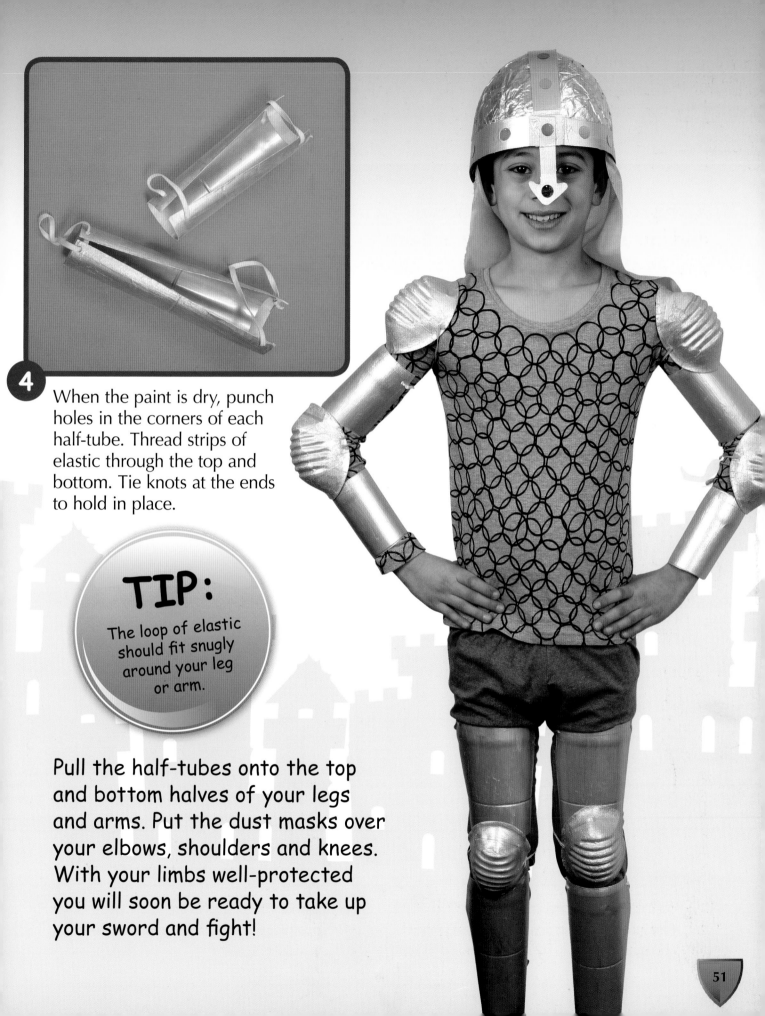

4

When the paint is dry, punch holes in the corners of each half-tube. Thread strips of elastic through the top and bottom. Tie knots at the ends to hold in place.

TIP:

The loop of elastic should fit snugly around your leg or arm.

Pull the half-tubes onto the top and bottom halves of your legs and arms. Put the dust masks over your elbows, shoulders and knees. With your limbs well-protected you will soon be ready to take up your sword and fight!

A TERRIFIC TABARD

A knight wore another piece of clothing over the top of the chain mail vest called a tabard. The tabard often had a symbol on the front.

1 Fold a pillowcase in half. Cut the corners off the closed end of the pillowcase as shown in the picture.

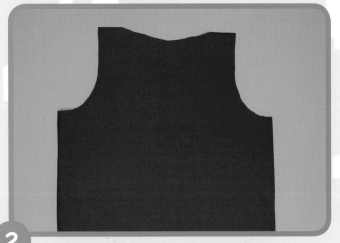

2 Unfold the pillowcase to check the size of the armholes and neck hole you have just made.

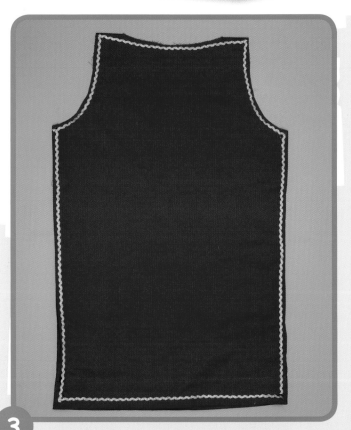

3 Glue gold ribbon around the edges of the pillowcase to make a border.

52

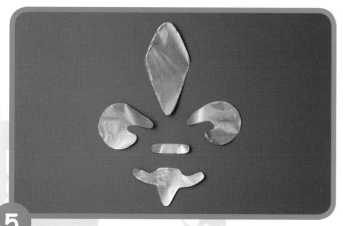

Now you are looking really smart, and fit for a place at the king's court!

4 Draw a symbol onto the back of the gold paper. The symbol could be a cross, a flower or an animal, such as a lion.

5 Cut the shape out.

6 Glue the shape onto the front of the pillowcase.

Knights wore gloves called gauntlets to protect their hands and arms in battle. Gauntlets sometimes had spikes on the wrists to make them look fearsome.

To make your gauntlets you will need:
Thin card
A pair of scissors
Black paint and a paintbrush
A silver pen
Craft glue and a paintbrush
A pen or pencil
A ruler
A pair of black gloves

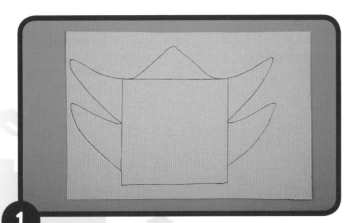

1 Draw a square slightly wider than your wrist onto card, about 10 x 10 cm (4 x 4 inches). Draw spikes coming out from the sides of the square and a triangle at one end.

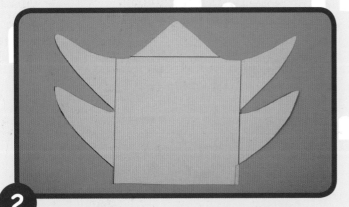

2 Cut the shape out. Use this shape as a template to cut out three more card shapes.

3 Paint all four shapes black.

4 Decorate two of the shapes using a silver pen.

5 Glue the edges of each plain shape to a decorated shape.

When the glue has dried, put on your gloves and slip the card shapes over the top. With these smart gauntlets you are ready for a bout of jousting!

A TRUSTY SWORD

Knights carried sharp, shiny swords which they used to battle with monsters.

1 Cut a long, thin rectangle of cardboard 60 x 6 cm (24 x 2 inches). Then cut out a narrow section at the bottom of the blade to make the handle. It should be the width of the cardboard tube and about 15 cm (6 inches) long.

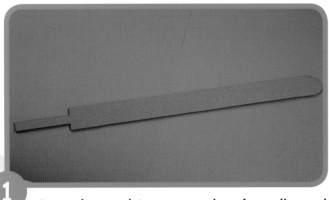

TIP: Make sure your blade has a rounded end. Otherwise it could be dangerous!

2 Cut two pointed pieces of cardboard 30 cm (12 inches) long and the same width as the tube. Glue them to the handle. Paint the blade silver.

3 Paint the cardboard tube gold and glue a plastic bottle top onto the end.

56

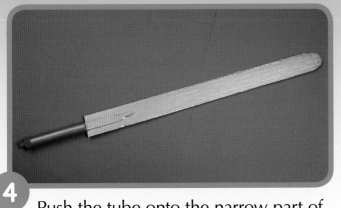

4 Push the tube onto the narrow part of the blade and glue it in place.

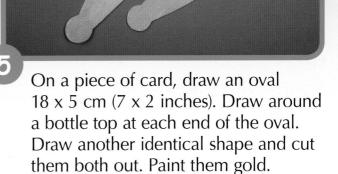

5 On a piece of card, draw an oval 18 x 5 cm (7 x 2 inches). Draw around a bottle top at each end of the oval. Draw another identical shape and cut them both out. Paint them gold.

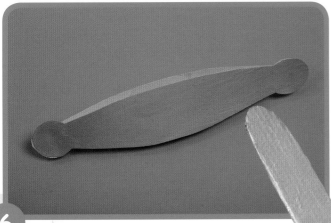

6 Glue the circles at the end of the shapes together to make the hilt.

Now you are ready to take on a dragon!

7 Push the hilt over the tube and glue in place where the handle meets the blade. Glue sequins onto each side of the hilt.

A DEFENSIVE SHIELD

Knights used large shields to protect themselves from their enemies' swords.

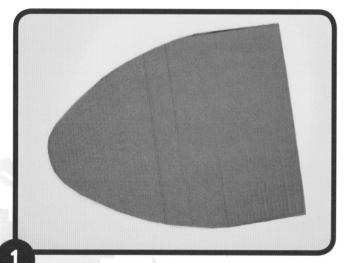

1 Draw a shield shape onto the cardboard and cut it out.

2 Paint the shield silver and the string gold. When the paint is dry, glue the string in a pattern around the edge of the shield.

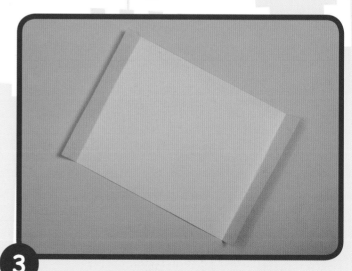

3 Cut a rectangle out of thin card 25 x 18 cm (10 x 7 inches). Fold a strip that is 1 cm (½ inch) wide along both of the shorter edges.

4

Glue the folded strips to the back of the shield, making a loop big enough to fit your arm through. This will allow you to hold the shield.

Knights often decorated their shield with a coat of arms. Find out how to do this next.

FAMILY PRIDE

A knight's shield bore a design called a coat of arms. This gave information about the history of the knight's family.

To make your own coat of arms you will need:
Paper
Card
A pair of scissors
Coloured paints and a paintbrush
A pen or pencil
Craft glue and a paintbrush

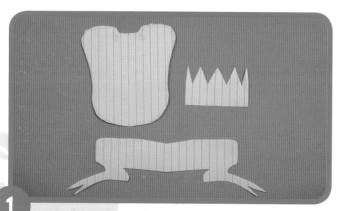

1 Fold a piece of paper in half and draw half a shield shape, a crown and a scroll. Cut them out and unfold the paper. Your shapes will be symmetrical.

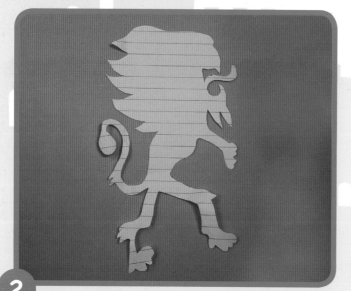

2 Draw a lion shape on paper and cut it out.

3 Draw around all of the paper shapes on card and cut them out. You will need to draw and cut out two lions.

You can find out if your family has a coat of arms on the Internet. If it does you could draw your own coat of arms and put it on your shield.

4 Draw a cross in the middle of the small shield to divide it into four sections. Paint the sections different colours.

5 Paint all the other shapes, too.

6 Glue all the shapes in the centre of your shield.

A LANCE FOR LIFE

Knights used to compete in jousting games. They charged at their opponent with a lance and tried to knock each other off their horse.

Make your own lance using:
Foam pipe insulation about 1m (3 feet) long
Coloured tape
Card
Silver paint and a paintbrush
Sequins
Craft glue and a paintbrush
A pair of scissors
A pen or pencil
A ruler

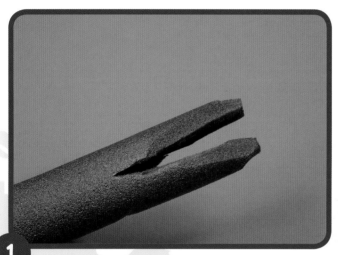

1 Cut a long, thin triangle out of one end of the foam pipe.

2 Stick coloured tape around the pipe at an angle. Use the tape to shape the cut end into a point.

TIP: You could use a small plate to draw around.

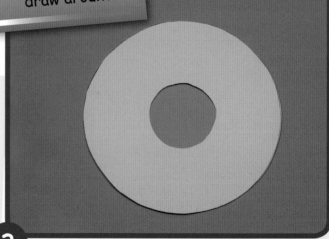

3 Draw a circle with a diameter of about 15 cm (6 inches) onto card. Cut it out. Then cut out a circle, the same size as the pipe, in the middle of the card.

What do you call a knight who can't stop fighting?
Sir Lance-a-lot!

4 Cut a small triangle out of the circle. Paint the shape silver.

5 Glue the two edges together to make a cone shape. Decorate it with sequins.

6 When the glue is dry, slip the ring onto the foam pipe to make a hand guard for your lance.

A BATTLE BANNER

Knights often carried flags into battle. The colours of their flag showed which side they were fighting for.

Make your own flag using:
1m (3 feet) of dowel pole
Coloured tape
Gold ribbon
A polystyrene ball
Gold paint and a paintbrush
Two lengths of material, each about 80 cm (30 inches) long
Craft glue and a paintbrush
A pair of scissors

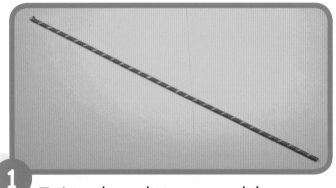

1 Twist coloured tape around the dowel pole.

2 Paint the polystyrene ball gold. Then ask an adult to help you to push it onto the end of the pole.

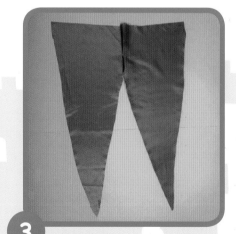

3 Cut a long triangle out of each length of material. Position the triangles so that one overlaps the other slightly at the widest point and glue them together.

4 Spread glue along the edges of the triangles and fold them over.

5 Fold the side edges of the triangles over by 3 cm (1 inch) and glue them in place.

6 Turn the material over and glue gold ribbon around the edges of the triangles.

7 Guide the dowel pole through the material tunnel.

Wave your flag proudly as you head off to fight for your king and country.

DRESSING UP AS A

This chapter shows you how to make a costume for a seafaring pirate captain. Learn how to make a pirate's hook and eye patch, a skull and crossbones hat and a trusty parrot friend!

PIRATE

TATTERED TOGS

Making a costume can be messy work! Make sure you cover all surfaces before you start with newspaper.

Pirates spent most of their time at sea. Their clothes became very dirty and tattered because they wore them every day.

Make your own pirate's trousers and t-shirt using:
A pair of old trousers
An old white t-shirt
Coloured felt
Fabric paints and a paintbrush
A marker pen
Craft glue and a paintbrush
A ruler
A pair of scissors
Newspaper

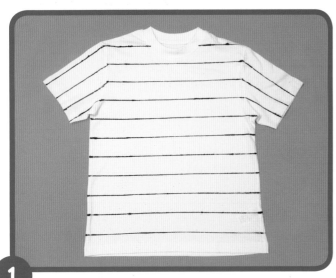

1 Use a ruler and marker pen to draw lines across your t-shirt.

TIP: Put newspaper inside the t-shirt so that the paint doesn't soak through to the other side.

2 Paint every other gap with fabric paint to make the clothing stripy.

3 Cut triangles along the edge of the sleeves and along the bottom of the t-shirt to make it look old and tattered.

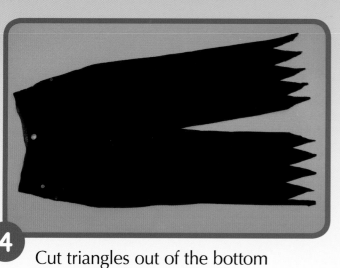

4 Cut triangles out of the bottom of the trouser legs, too.

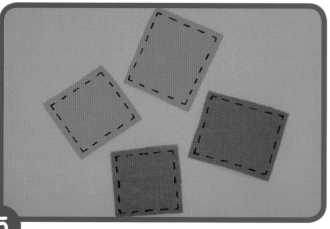

5 Cut some 10 cm (4 inch) square patches out of felt. Draw stitches around the edge of the patches with fabric paint.

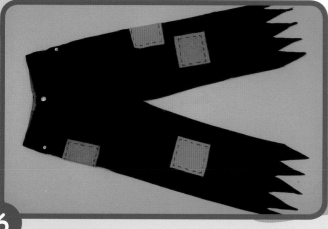

6 Glue the patches onto the trousers using craft glue.

Now you are ready for life onboard the pirate ship. Be prepared to work hard!

A WELL-WORN WAISTCOAT

Pirates often put on a waistcoat to look smart. Over time the waistcoat became as tatty as the pirates' other clothes.

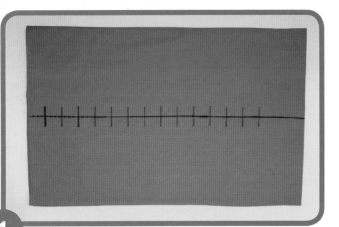

1 Draw a straight line up the middle of the pillowcase using a marker pen and ruler. Carefully draw stitches across the line.

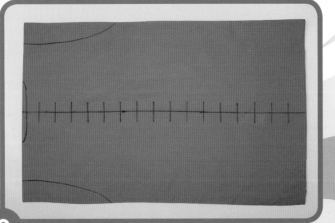

2 Draw lines to mark the holes for your head and arms as shown in this picture.

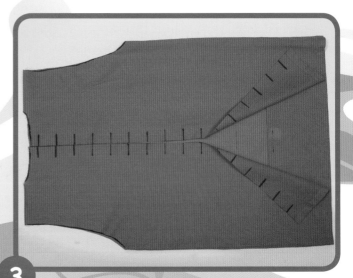

3 Use scissors to cut along the lines to make the holes. Then cut along the middle line through the front piece of fabric only. You will then be able to open your waistcoat.

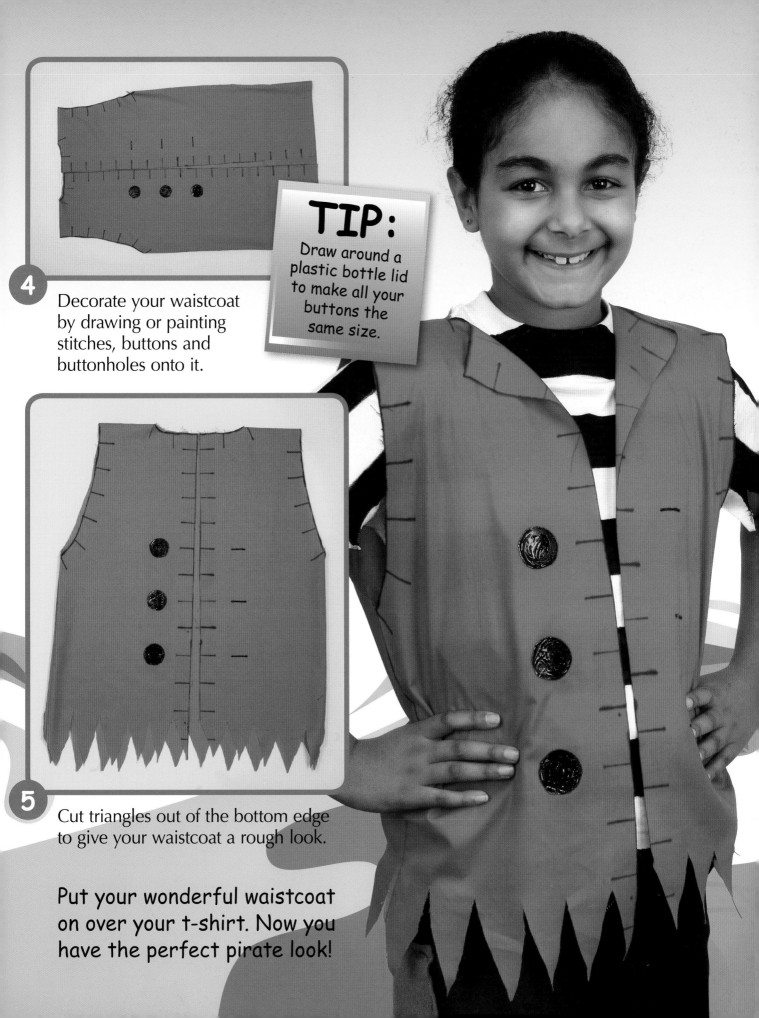

4 Decorate your waistcoat by drawing or painting stitches, buttons and buttonholes onto it.

TIP: Draw around a plastic bottle lid to make all your buttons the same size.

5 Cut triangles out of the bottom edge to give your waistcoat a rough look.

Put your wonderful waistcoat on over your t-shirt. Now you have the perfect pirate look!

A BRILLIANT BANDANA

Pirates worked hard in the sun all day. They wore bandanas around their heads to soak up sweat.

To make a bandana you will need:
A 60 cm (24 inch) square piece of red fabric
A marker pen
Fabric paints and a paintbrush

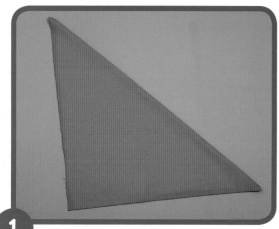

1 Fold your red fabric in half so that it looks like a triangle.

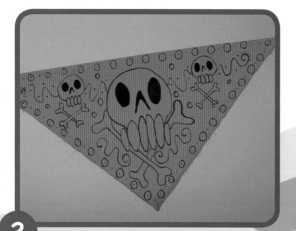

2 Draw patterns onto the fabric using a marker pen. You could draw skulls, lines, dots or squiggles.

3 Decorate the fabric using fabric paint.

With your bandana in place you're ready to work. But remember that pirates had lots of fun, too!

EYE, EYE, CAPTAIN!

Pirates were a rowdy bunch and often had fights. If pirates injured an eye, they would wear an eyepatch.

Make your own eyepatch using:
A piece of black felt or thin black card
A piece of black elastic
A pair of scissors
A ruler

1 Cut out a rounded triangle from the felt or thin card.

2 Fold 1 cm (½ inch) of a corner over. Snip a small slit in the middle of the fold.

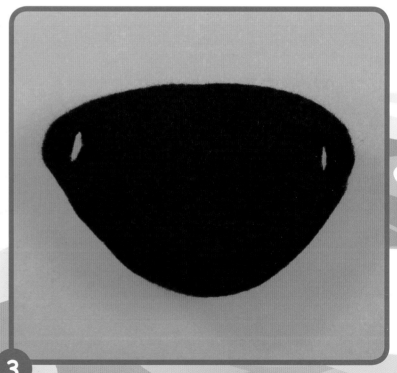

3 Repeat step two with the other corner.

4 Wrap a piece of elastic around your head to measure the length you need. Remove the elastic from your head and cut it to length. Then thread the elastic through the slits and knot it at each end.

With your eyepatch in place, you'll look like a really tough pirate!

HATS OFF TO PIRATES

Pirate chiefs wore hats showing the skull and crossbones to scare their enemies – and their crew!

TIP:
If you don't have sugar paper, you could use thin card.

1 Fold the sugar paper into a long strip. Measure around your head with a tape measure and cut the strip to the right length. Tape the ends together.

To make your own pirate hat you will need:
Black sugar paper
A tape measure
A pair of scissors
Sticky tape
Thin black card
A pen or pencil
A craft knife
White paint
Craft glue and a paintbrush
Sponge
Gold ribbon

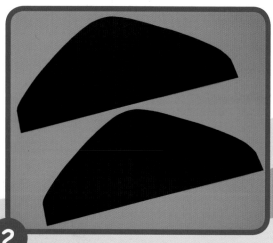

2 Cut two rounded triangles out of thin black card, about 40 cm (16 inches) long.

TIP:
The eye sockets in the stencil must join the outer edge.

3 Draw a skull and crossbones onto card to make a stencil. Ask an adult to help you cut it out using a craft knife.

Now that you've finished making your pirate hat, you'd better get used to bossing people around. Only the fiercest pirate chiefs can wear hats like this one.

4 Sponge white paint through the stencil onto one of the rounded triangles.

5 Glue gold ribbon around the edges of the triangle.

6 Use glue or sticky tape to attach the triangles to the front and back of the sugar paper ring. Glue the edges of the rounded triangles together.

BY HOOK OR BY CROOK

Accidents on board ship were common. If you were out at sea and lost a hand, it would be replaced with a hook.

Make your own hook using:
A large plastic bottle
A pair of scissors
Craft glue and a paintbrush
Newspaper
Black paint and a paintbrush
Silver paint and a paintbrush
Cardboard
String
Split pins
A ruler

1 Ask an adult to cut off the top of the plastic bottle. Using glue, cover it in pieces of newspaper. Make sure you cover the sharp edge.

2 When the glue is dry, paint the bottle black.

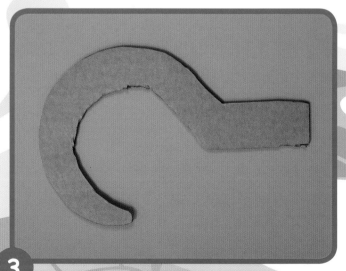

3 Draw a hook shape on a piece of cardboard. Draw a strip underneath the hook about 10 cm (4 inches) long and the same width as the bottleneck. Cut the shape out.

It's not easy using a hook instead of your hand. A pirate's life was hard!

4

Paint the hook silver.

TIP:
Make sure that the handle reaches down into the bottle top so that you can hold onto it.

5

Push the strip into the bottleneck. Cover the join with newspaper dipped in glue. When the glue dries, paint over the join.

6

Glue string in a zigzag at the bottom of the bottle top. Push split pins in between the string to look like gold studs.

Life could be lonely at sea. Pirates used to keep parrots to entertain them on long voyages.

Make your own parrot using:

An old red sock
Old pairs of tights or socks
Yellow pipe cleaners
Craft glue and a paintbrush
A pair of scissors
Coloured felt
Plastic eyes
Coloured feathers
A ruler

1 Stuff the sock with tights or socks to make the parrot's body. Place three pipe cleaners at the bottom. Glue the gap to hold the pipe cleaners in place.

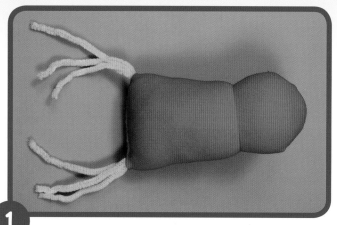

TIP:
You might need to add an extra pipe cleaner to make the ring big enough.

2 Bend the pipe cleaners around to make a ring that is big enough to fit onto your shoulder. Twist the pipe cleaners together.

3 Cut a mask shape out of a piece of felt, about 10 cm (4 inches) wide. Glue on plastic eyes. Then cut a 10 cm (4 inch) semicircle out of yellow felt. Glue the middle of the semicircle onto the mask between the eyes.

4

Fold the semicircle and glue the sides together to make a beak. Glue the mask onto the parrot's head.

5

Glue colourful feathers onto the back of the parrot's body.

6

Cut wing shapes out of felt in different sizes and colours. Glue the shapes on top of each other.

You'll never be lonely with Polly the Parrot to keep you company. Perhaps you could teach her to say your name!

7

Glue the wings onto the parrot's body.

8

Twist two pipe cleaners around the ring. Shape them to make the parrot's feet.

LAND AHOY!

Pirates needed to see into the distance. They used a telescope to spot faraway lands and enemy ships approaching.

To make your own telescope you will need:
Thin black card
A pair of scissors
A ruler
Gold paint and a paintbrush
A hole punch
Split pins
Craft glue and a paintbrush
Clothes pegs

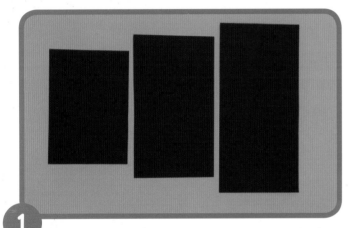

1 Cut three rectangles out of thin black card. The first rectangle should be 14 x 10 cm (5 x 4 inches), the second rectangle 16 x 10 cm (6 x 4 inches) and the third 18 x 10 cm (7 x 4 inches).

2 Paint a gold strip that is 1 cm (½ inch) wide along the longest edges of each rectangle.

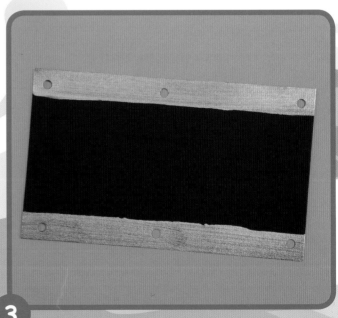

3 Punch three holes along each long edge of the medium-sized rectangle.

Now you can see for miles and miles! When you spot land, remember to shout 'Land ahoy!'

4 Punch three holes along one long edge of the smallest and largest rectangles.

5 Roll each rectangle into a tube so the holes match up. Glue in place.

TIP: Use clothes pegs to hold the tubes in place while the glue dries.

6 Join the three tubes together by pushing gold split pins through the holes.

A TRUSTY CUTLASS

Pirates loved to fight! One of their favourite weapons was a curved sword called a cutlass.

1 The cardboard tube will be the cutlass handle. Paint a 7 cm (3 inch) length with glue and wind string around it.

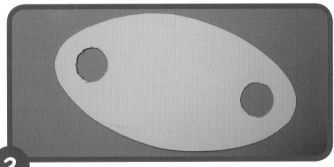

2 Cut an oval out of card to make a guard. It should be around 25 cm (10 inches) wide. Draw around the cardboard tube and cut holes at each end of the oval.

3 Paint the guard gold.

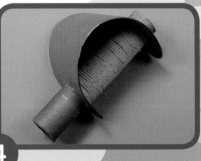

4 Thread the cardboard tube through the holes in the guard.

5 Push a plastic bottle lid onto one end of the tube and glue in place.

Now that you have your cutlass, you're ready to be a fearsome pirate. Just be careful who you pick a fight with – pirates can be really mean!

6 Draw the shape of your blade onto cardboard. The narrow end should not be wider than the cardboard tube.

7 Cut the blade out and paint it silver.

TIP:
Use clothes pegs to hold the blade in place while the glue dries.

8 Cut two lines down the sides of the cardboard tube above your guard. Push your blade inside and glue in place. Cover any gaps with newspaper and glue. Paint when dry.

X MARKS THE SPOT

Pirates buried their treasure to keep it secret from other pirates. They made maps to help them find the booty again when they needed it.

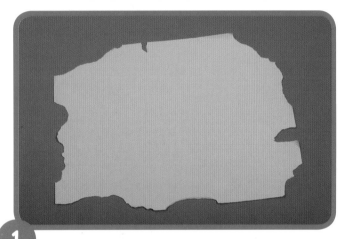

1 Tear the edges of the paper to make it look old.

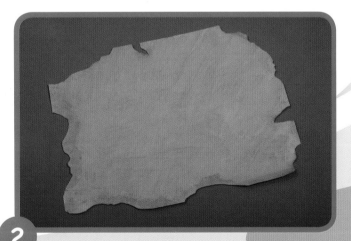

2 Stain the paper by rubbing a cold, wet teabag over it. Let it dry.

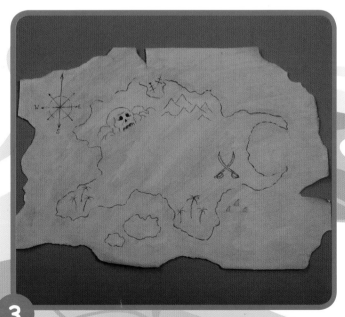

3 Draw a map of the island where your treasure is buried. You could draw some mountains and trees on the island, and a compass so you know which direction is north.

4 Mark your treasure with a red X.
Draw a path to the treasure, too.

Keep your treasure
map somewhere safe,
where no other pirates
will ever find it!

DRESSING UP AS A

This chapter shows you how to make a gorgeous ball gown with slippers and a sash. Dressed up in your tiara and jewellery you will be ready to dazzle everyone at the palace ball!

PRINCESS

A GORGEOUS GOWN

Making a costume can be messy work! Make sure you cover all surfaces with newspaper before you start.

One of the best things about being a princess is having lots of lovely dresses. This gorgeous ball gown is for wearing on very special occasions.

To make your own gown you will need:

An old t-shirt
A ruler
A compass
Sparkly net fabric about 1m (3 feet) long
A pair of scissors
A pen or pencil
A needle
Cotton thread
Craft gems
Craft glue and a paintbrush
A strip of fabric to fit around your waist
An old lace or net curtain

1 Measure the join between the body of the t-shirt and the sleeve, from shoulder to underarm. Double the length and set your compass to that size.

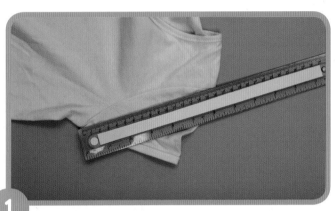

2 Use the compass to draw a semicircle onto the sparkly net. Cut the semicircle out. Then repeat so that you have two semicircles.

TIP:

If you cannot draw onto your material, draw the semicircle onto a piece of paper. Cut the semicircle out and pin it to the material. Then use it as a template to cut around.

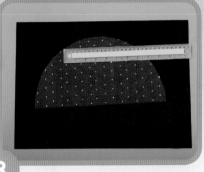

3 Measure the width of the t-shirt join (from step 1) straight across the curved edge of each semicircle and mark.

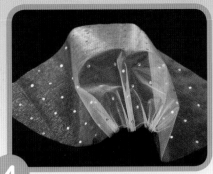

4 Sew around the curved edge between the two marks you have made. Try to make all of your stitches the same length. Then pull the cotton so that the material pleats and tie a knot.

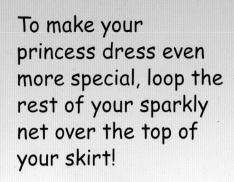

To make your princess dress even more special, loop the rest of your sparkly net over the top of your skirt!

5 Sew the bottom corners of each semicircle to the t-shirt where the underarm joins the body. Then sew over the pleats to join the pleated section to the shoulder of the t-shirt.

6 Glue craft gems around the neck of the t-shirt.

7 Tie a strip of fabric around your waist. Loop the lace or net curtain over the fabric strip to make a skirt.

A STUNNING SASH

A stunning sash will make a princess's ball gown look even more special. You could make several sashes in different colours to wear on different occasions.

To make your own sash you will need:
A strip of coloured material about 1m (3 feet) long
A craft knife
A piece of cardboard
A ruler
Gold paint and a paintbrush
A pen or pencil
Craft glue and a paintbrush
Craft gems

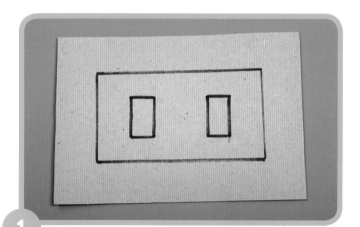

1 With a ruler draw a rectangle about 8 x 16 cm (3 x 6 inches) on cardboard. Draw two smaller rectangles inside the large one.

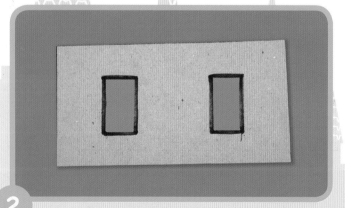

2 Ask an adult to cut out the rectangle with a craft knife. Then cut out the smaller rectangles to make a buckle.

3 Paint your buckle gold. You could also glue on some craft gems if you like.

4

Thread the material strip through the buckle so the gold side is showing. The buckle should be in the middle of the material.

Tie the material around your waist in a bow at the back or at the side. The sash will hold your dress together and make it look beautiful!

DAINTY TOES

As a princess you will be invited to dance at lots of balls. Like Cinderella you will want to wear pretty slippers – but perhaps not made of glass!

To make your slippers you will need:
A pair of ballet shoes
Ribbon
Craft glue and a paintbrush
Shiny beads
Craft gems
A needle

TIP:
If your shoes are hard to sew through, ask an adult to make holes in them. Then you can thread the ribbon through the holes.

1 Glue the gems or beads onto your shoes using craft glue.

2 Carefully sew ribbon along the edges of the opening in a criss-cross pattern.

3 Put your shoes on and wrap the ribbons around your legs. Then tie them in a bow.

You will be able to dance all night in these beautiful slippers.

GLAMOROUS GLOVES

Princesses like to be very fashionable. To be a really stylish princess you will need a pair of long, elegant gloves.

You can make your own gloves using:
A pair of white, footless tights
A pair of scissors
Two craft gems
Craft glue and a paintbrush
Thin, coloured ribbon
A needle
Thin elastic

1 Cut the legs off the tights.

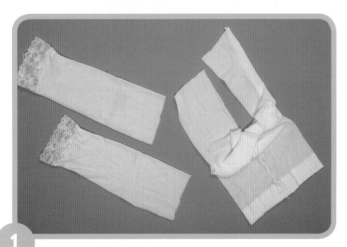

TIP:
If you do not have footless tights, cut the feet off the legs as well. Then turn the edge over and sew that too.

2 Turn over the top edge of each leg and sew big stitches of elastic around it. Pull tight and tie the elastic in a bow.

3 Glue a gem in the middle at one end of each glove.

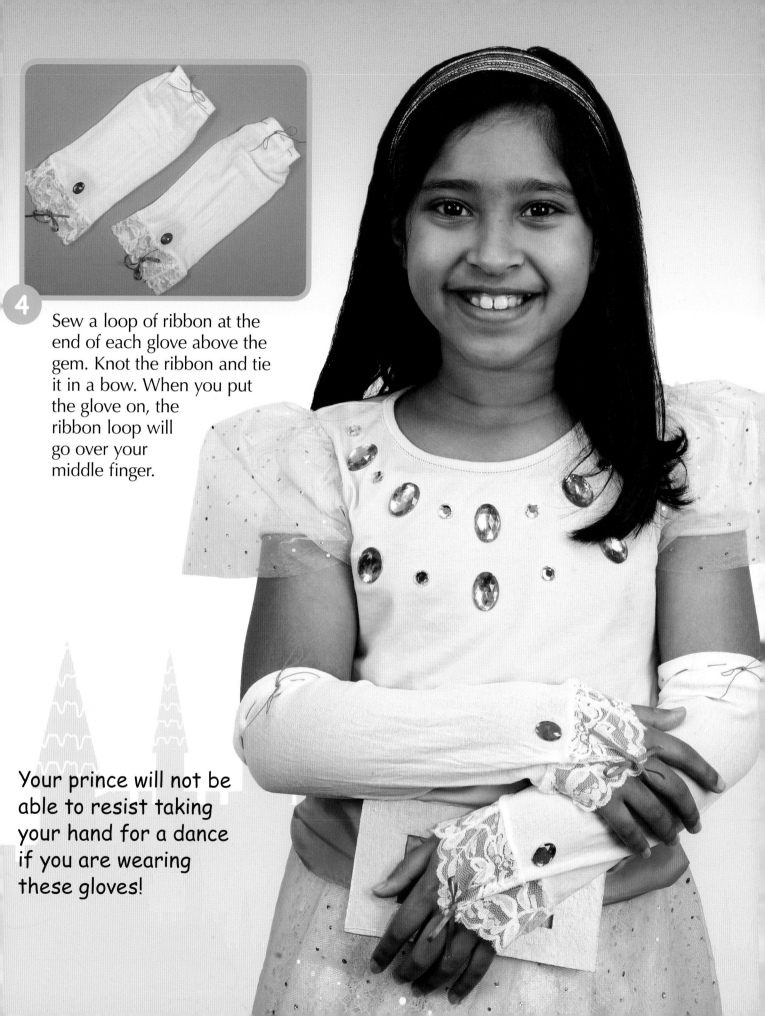

4 Sew a loop of ribbon at the end of each glove above the gem. Knot the ribbon and tie it in a bow. When you put the glove on, the ribbon loop will go over your middle finger.

Your prince will not be able to resist taking your hand for a dance if you are wearing these gloves!

A COURTLY CLOAK

During the winter months a princess must keep warm. A cloak is like a coat or a blanket that can be worn over your fine clothes.

1 Cut the material into a rectangle about 100 x 150 cm (40 x 60 inches). Sew a piece of ribbon along one of the shorter edges of the rectangle.

2 Mark a point about 40 cm (16 inches) in from the centre of the ribbon. Sew some more ribbon from the edges to this point in a V-shape.

3 Pull the ribbon slightly and then knot either side. This will make the hood of your cloak.

4 Use the ribbon to loosely tie the cloak around your neck.

When you leave the ball at midnight your cloak will keep you warm and cosy!

TO CROWN IT ALL

A princess has a beautiful crown to wear on her head. This crown is called a tiara.

1 On card draw an outline of the tiara and cut it out. The tiara should be about 25 cm (10 inches) long.

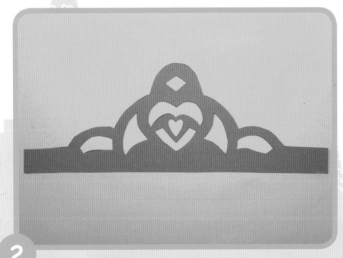

2 Draw symmetrical shapes on the card. Ask an adult to cut them out with a craft knife.

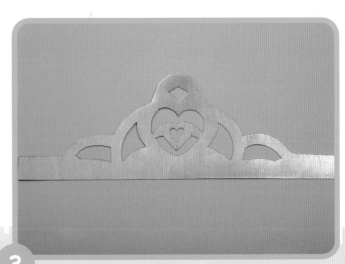

3 Paint the tiara silver.

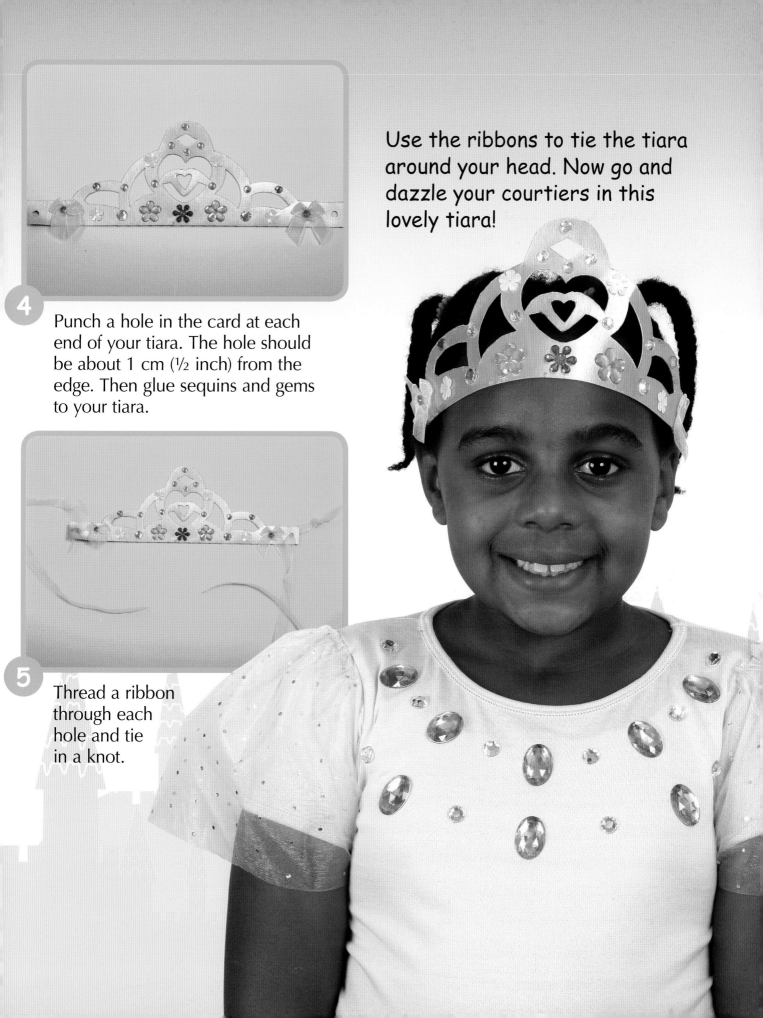

4 Punch a hole in the card at each end of your tiara. The hole should be about 1 cm (½ inch) from the edge. Then glue sequins and gems to your tiara.

5 Thread a ribbon through each hole and tie in a knot.

Use the ribbons to tie the tiara around your head. Now go and dazzle your courtiers in this lovely tiara!

ALL THAT GLITTERS

Princesses have lots of jewellery. The bigger and sparklier the better!

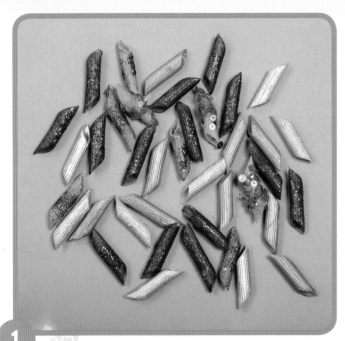

1 Pour the glue, paint, sequins and glitter into separate plastic trays. Then roll the pasta in the trays.

TIP:
If you want your pasta pieces to look different, roll some of them in the paint only, some of them in the paint and glitter trays, and some of them in the glue and sequin trays.

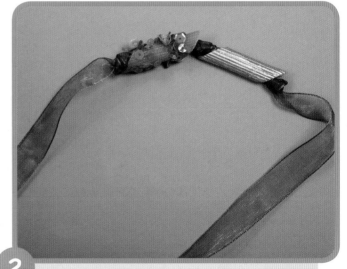

2 Cut two lengths of ribbon, 60 cm (24 inches) long and 40 cm (16 inches) long. When the pasta has dried, thread the pieces onto the ribbons. Tie knots between the pieces of pasta.

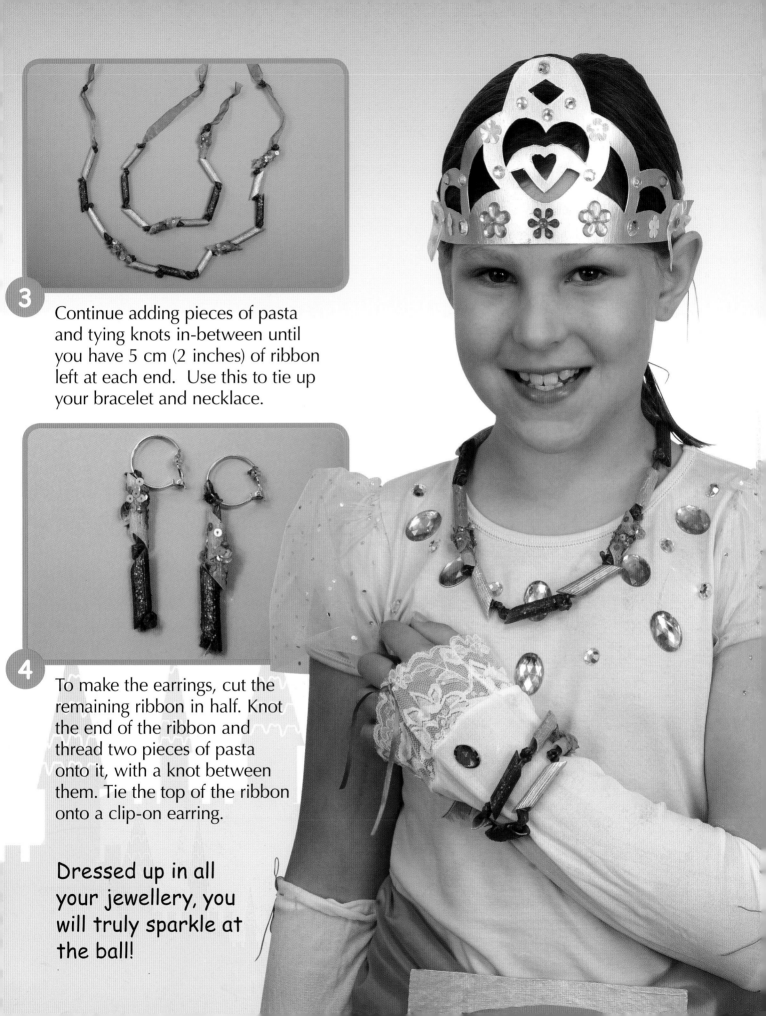

3 Continue adding pieces of pasta and tying knots in-between until you have 5 cm (2 inches) of ribbon left at each end. Use this to tie up your bracelet and necklace.

4 To make the earrings, cut the remaining ribbon in half. Knot the end of the ribbon and thread two pieces of pasta onto it, with a knot between them. Tie the top of the ribbon onto a clip-on earring.

Dressed up in all your jewellery, you will truly sparkle at the ball!

A BEJEWELLED BROOCH

A brooch is like a badge covered with lots of jewels. This beautiful brooch is the finishing touch to a princess's jewellery.

To make your own princess brooch you will need:
Cardboard
A ruler
Silver paint and a paintbrush
A pair of scissors
Sequins
A safety pin
Craft gems
Sticky tape
Craft glue and a paintbrush
Glitter
A pen or pencil

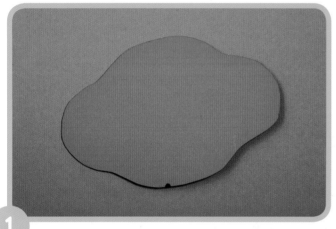

1 Draw the shape of your brooch onto cardboard and cut it out. The brooch should be about 10 cm (4 inches) long.

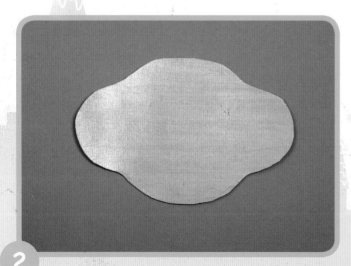

2 Paint the brooch silver.

3 Decorate your brooch with sequins, gems and glitter.

4

Stick a safety pin to the back of
your brooch using sticky tape.

Wear this brooch
to show everyone
what a wealthy and
fashionable princess
you are!

TIP:
Use your brooch
to fasten your
cloak.

A HEAVENLY HAT

Princesses do not wear their tiaras all the time. When they go travelling or out to watch tournaments they need a suitable hat.

To make your own hat you will need:
Coloured card
A pair of scissors
Ribbon or strips of fabric
Craft glue and a paintbrush
Coloured paint and a paintbrush
A pen or pencil
Sequins
A ruler
Elastic
A hole punch

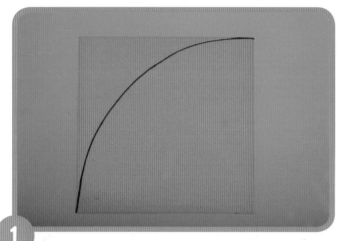

1 Draw a quarter circle onto coloured card. The straight sides should be about 25 cm (10 inches) long.

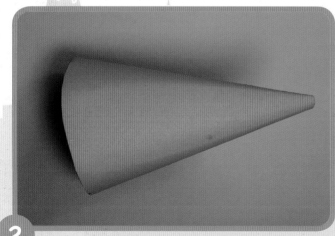

2 Cut out the quarter circle and glue it together to make a cone shape. Cut the top off the cone to make a hole.

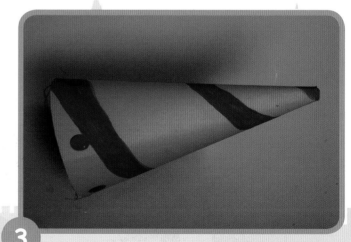

3 Paint a spiral down the cone and glue sequins at the bottom.

This hat will make you look like a truly magical princess!

4 Punch a hole at the bottom of the hat on either side. Thread a piece of elastic through the holes. The elastic will go under your chin to hold your hat on.

5 Cut strips of fabric or ribbon about 80 cm (30 inches) long. Knot them together at one end.

6 Push the knot through the hole in the top of the hat, leaving the ribbons outside. Glue the knot in place.

Every princess needs a handsome prince to meet at a ball.

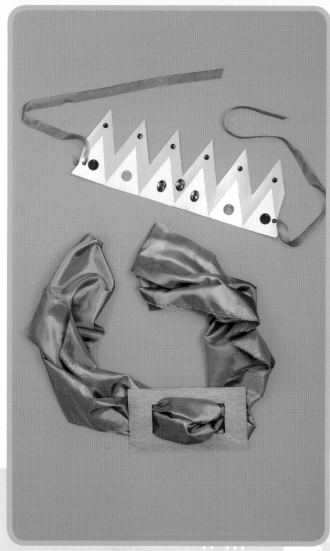

Use the instructions for the princess sash and tiara to make a prince's belt and crown. You might choose to paint the prince's crown gold and use gold or blue material for the belt.

A prince would wear a smart waistcoat to the ball. Make your own using:

A blue pillowcase

Coloured tape

A marker pen

A pair of scissors

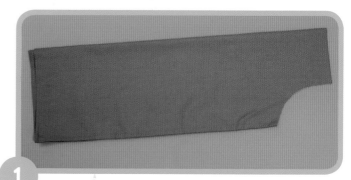

1 Fold the pillowcase in half. Cut a quarter circle in the top corner that is not folded to make the armholes.

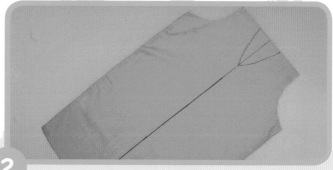

2 Unfold the pillowcase. Draw a line up the centre and a V-shape at the top for the neckline.

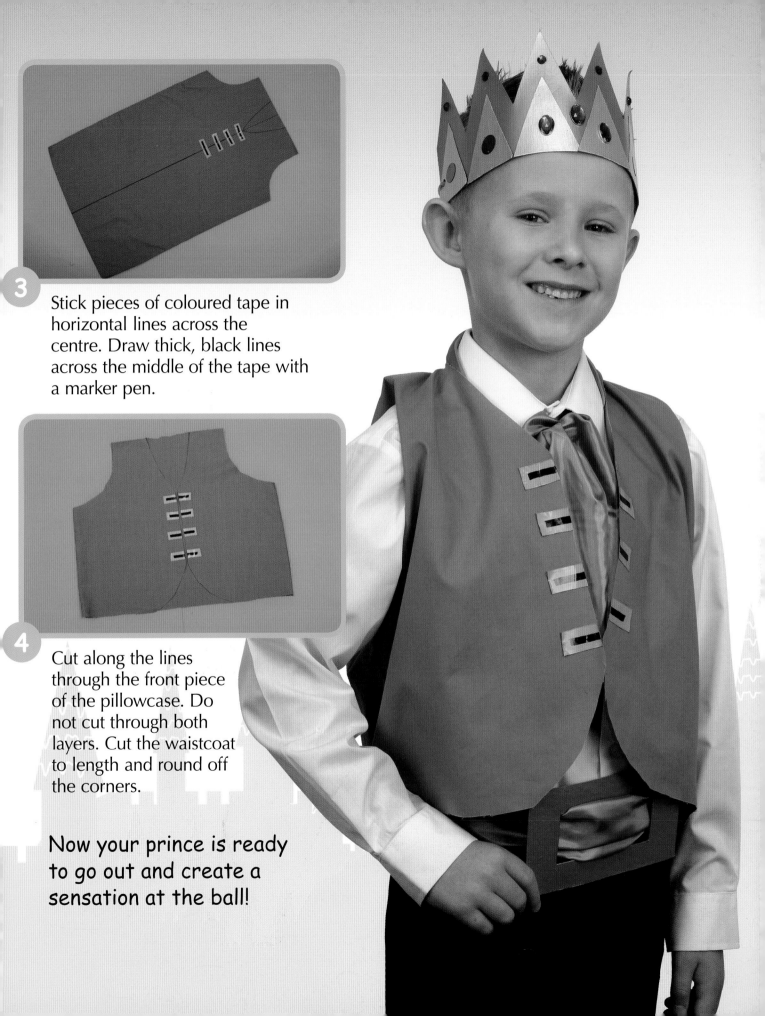

3 Stick pieces of coloured tape in horizontal lines across the centre. Draw thick, black lines across the middle of the tape with a marker pen.

4 Cut along the lines through the front piece of the pillowcase. Do not cut through both layers. Cut the waistcoat to length and round off the corners.

Now your prince is ready to go out and create a sensation at the ball!

DRESSING UP AS A

This chapter shows you how to make a high-tech 'robody' loaded with gadgets, gizmos and flashing lights. You can even make your own mechanical arms for those tricky jobs that only a robot can do.

ROBOT

ROBODY

Robots are very powerful machines. Their power source is stored in their upper bodies.

Make your own protective casing using:
A large cardboard box that will fit over your chest
A pair of scissors
Coloured paints and a paintbrush
A ruler
A black marker pen
Cardboard
Gold elastic

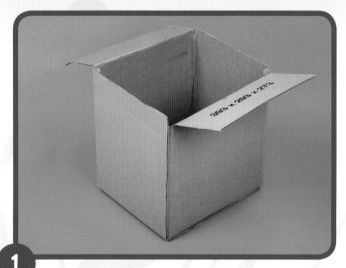

1 Open up the top of the cardboard box and cut the flaps off two opposite sides.

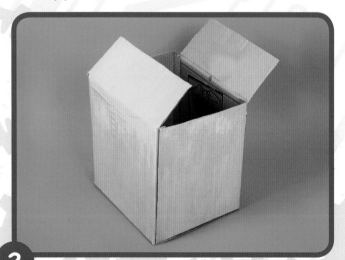

2 Open up the bottom of the box and paint the whole box in one colour.

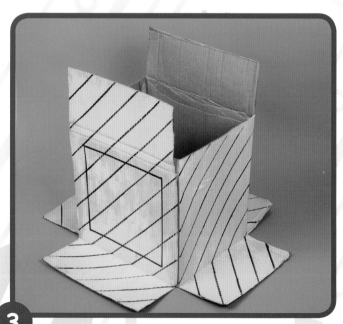

3 Using a ruler and a marker pen, draw diagonal lines across the box. Draw a large square on the front.

112

4 Paint in between the lines to make the box striped. Paint the square too.

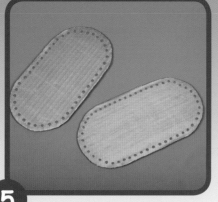

5 Cut two oval shapes out of cardboard, approximately 12 cm (5 inches) long and 6 cm (2 inches) wide. Paint them and add some dots around the edges. These will be the robot's shoulders.

6 Make two small holes 4 cm (1 inch) apart on each end of the strips.

7 Make two holes in each corner of the two flaps at the top of the box.

8 Use gold elastic to attach the shoulders to the flaps.

Now that you've made your robot body, get ready to decorate it!

 # GADGETS AND GIZMOS

A robot has many different displays and dials on its body. Make a set using shiny and brightly coloured things.

Make different gadgets and swap them around using:
Coloured card
Gold paper
A pair of scissors
A pen or pencil
Craft glue and a paintbrush
Split pins
Fun foam
Wool and five buttons
Velcro
Sequins
A ruler
A compass

1 Cut a semicircle out of coloured card. Decorate it with strips of gold paper.

2 Use a compass to draw a circle on the back of another piece of card. Then draw shapes around the edge of the circle to make a cog-wheel.

3 Cut the cog out and decorate the coloured side with sequins.

With your control panels and gadgets working you can get ready for some robo-action!

4 Use a split pin to attach the cog to the semicircle. This allows the cog to spin around.

5 Cut a piece of fun foam into a rectangle 15 x 7 cm (6 x 3 inches). Ask an adult to help you make five pairs of holes in the foam. Each pair should be 5 cm (2 inches) apart.

TIP:
Attach your gadgets to your robot's body with Velcro. Think up some other gadgets you could make and attach.

6 Thread buttons onto pieces of wool. Thread the wool through the holes in the foam and tie a knot at the back. The buttons will slide up and down the wool.

INFORMATION OVERLOAD

A robot's body has many tubes to carry wires from one part of its body to another. Lots of information is passed along these wires.

To make your robot's tubes you will need:

1m (3 feet) of silver foam pipe insulation (lagging)

A pair of scissors

A craft knife

A biro

Plastic craft string

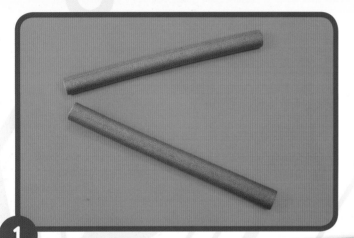

1 Cut the foam pipe in half.

TIP:
The holes should be slightly smaller than the end of the foam pipe. If the holes are too big, the pipe will not stay in place.

2 Ask an adult to cut two circles in each side of your robot's body.

3 Push the foam pipe through the holes.

4

Use a biro to make six holes in the box between the foam pipes.

5

Thread plastic craft string through the holes and tie together inside.

Now you are ready to do some serious calculations!

LIGHT ME UP

Robots often have flashing lights. They use the lights to flash warnings and coded messages to each other.

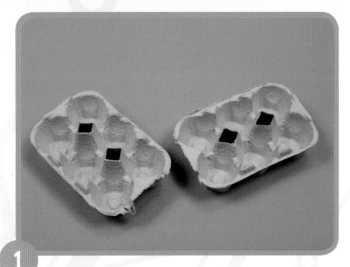

1 Cut off the points inside the egg box halves.

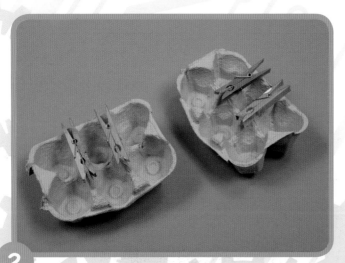

2 Glue the edges of the holes together to close the gaps. Hold in place with clothes pegs until the glue dries.

3 Paint the egg boxes. Decorate them with sequins and dots of a different coloured paint.

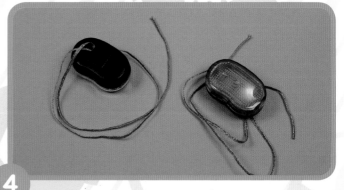

4 Tie gold elastic around the clips at the back of the bicycle lights.

Everyone will see you coming in your robot costume now!

TIP:
Make sure that you can still reach the button to turn the lights on!

5 Attach the lights to the egg boxes by tying the gold elastic down their centres.

6 Ask an adult to help you make holes in the middle of each side of the egg boxes.

7 Thread some more gold elastic through the holes and tie around the robot's shoulders.

BRAIN POWER

A robot's head is where it receives its messages. It needs a strong antenna to carry information to its computer 'brain'.

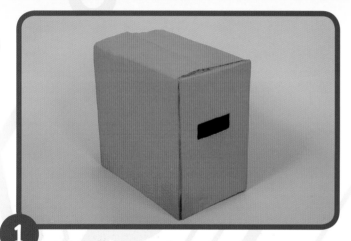

1 Ask an adult to help you cut out a rectangle in the box, about 15 x 7 cm (6 x 3 inches). This is the eye-hole. Then paint the box.

2 When the paint is dry, decorate your robot's face with sequins, paint and coloured paper.

3 Paint two egg box lids and two bottle lids. Use coloured paper, paint and sequins to decorate them.

Now you can look and think like a robot!

4 Ask an adult to cut the top off an empty plastic bottle. Then cover it with newspaper strips and glue.

5 Paint the bottle top and glue it to the top of the box. Glue the bottle lids to the egg box lids and glue onto each side of the box.

6 Thread the pipe cleaners into the straws. Bend the pipe cleaners to make an antenna shape. Insert the antenna into the plastic bottle top and glue in place.

ROBO-LEGS

A robot's body and head can be very heavy, so robots need to have strong, sturdy legs.

Make robo-legs using:
Two plastic bottles (square-shaped bottles if possible)
A craft knife
Masking tape
Coloured paint and a paintbrush
A hole-punch
Elastic
Two egg box bottom halves
Sequins
A pair of scissors
Craft glue and a paintbrush

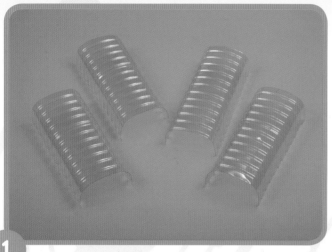

1 Ask an adult to cut the top and bottom off the empty plastic bottles. Then cut the bottles in half lengthways.

TIP: The loop of elastic should fit snugly around your leg.

2 Cover all of the edges with masking tape then paint the half-bottles.

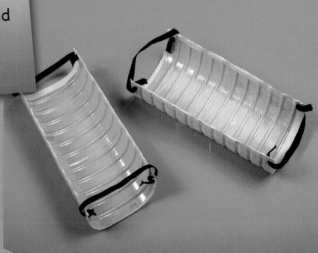

3 Punch holes in each corner of the half-bottles. Thread elastic through the holes and knot each end.

4 Cut the points out of the egg boxes and glue the gaps (as on page 118). Then paint them and decorate with paint and sequins.

5 Make a hole in the middle at each side of the egg boxes. Thread elastic through the holes and knot to make a loop.

Now your robo-legs are ready to wear! Pull the half-tubes onto the top and bottom halves of your legs. Put the egg boxes over your knees.

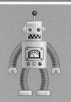

WELL-ARMED

Robots are very good at doing difficult jobs. They need special, mechanical arms to help them to do their work.

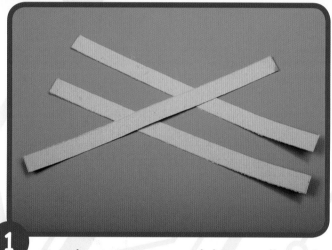

1 Cut three strips out of thin cardboard, about 2 x 30 cm (1 x 12 inches).

2 Take an empty crisp tube and wrap two of the card strips around its middle. Glue them in place.

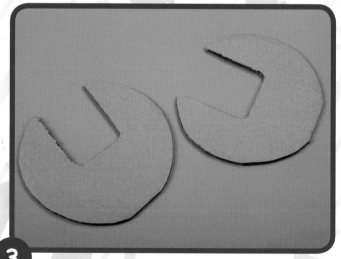

3 Ask an adult to cut two spanner head shapes, 15 cm (6 inches) wide, out of thick cardboard using a craft knife.

4 Stick the two spanner shapes together with masking tape. Fold the third card strip in half and tape it in place as the handle.

5 Ask an adult to cut the bottom off two plastic bottles with a craft knife. Cover the edges in masking tape.

Your robot arm tools are ready to wear. Hold on to the strips of cardboard inside the bottles.

6 Attach the spanner and hammer to the bottles by pushing the card handles into the necks of the bottles. Use masking tape to secure them.

7 Paint the bottles and glue metallic paper over the hammer and spanner shapes.

BEST FOOT FORWARD

Robots wear big, clumpy shoes and move slowly but steadily in them.

To make your robot shoes you will need:
Two rectangular tissue boxes
Coloured paints and a paintbrush
A ruler
A marker pen
Elastic

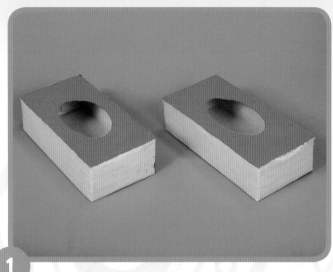

1 Paint the top and sides of two empty tissue boxes.

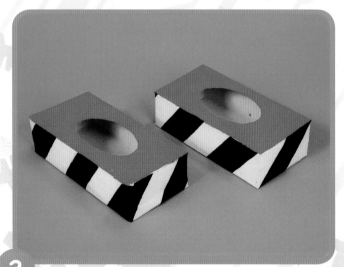

2 Use a ruler and marker pen to draw stripes around the sides of the boxes. Then paint stripes in.

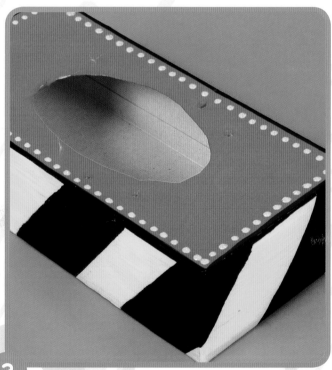

3 Add some dots of paint. Make two pairs of small holes either side of the large hole in each box.

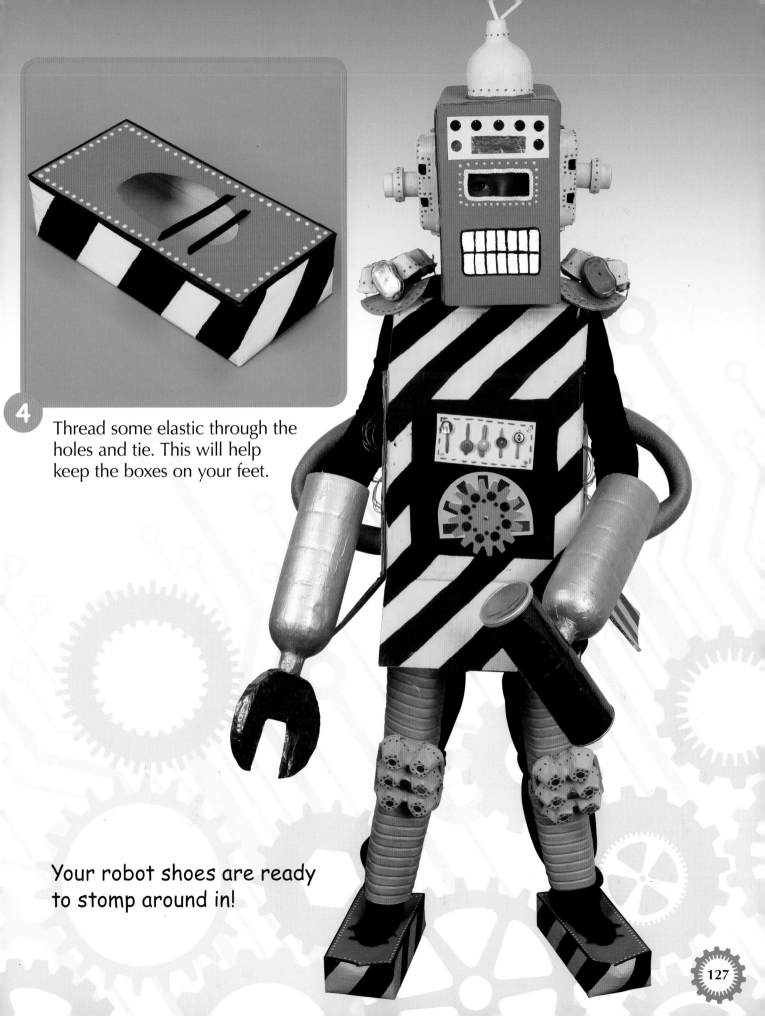

4 Thread some elastic through the holes and tie. This will help keep the boxes on your feet.

Your robot shoes are ready to stomp around in!

NOW LET'S HAVE A DRESSING UP PARTY!